D0232661

# The Zucchini and Carrot Cookbook

Illustrations by Shelley Adler

# The Zucchini and Carrot Cookbook

## Ruth Conrad Bateman

a Ward Ritchie Press book
distributed by Crown Publishers, Inc.
New York

Other Books by the Author

I Love To Cook Book

Serve It Cold!
(with June Crosby)

Fifty Great Buffet Parties

Copyright © 1976 by Ruth Conrad Bateman

All rights reserved.

No part of this book may be reproduced
in any form or by any means without
permission in writing from Ward Ritchie Press,
% Crown Publishers, Inc.
One Park Avenue, New York, New York 10016

Library of Congress Catalog Card Number: 75-41818
ISBN: 0-517-537710

10  9  8  7  6  5

Printed in the United States of America

# Acknowledgments

It is impossible to single out and name all of you good neighbors and friends who have given me recipes and ideas for this book. But I do thank each of you sincerely and hope you like the way I've handled your welcome suggestions.

I am especially grateful to Joan Henderson and Les Hubbard of Western Growers Association in Newport Beach, California for their help with sources, recipes, and ideas. I found the books from their Holtville Carrot Carnivals extremely interesting and helpful. All the recipes used have been tested and revised or updated, as necessary, to fit today's products and life-styles.

I sincerely appreciate Angela Burkle's help in rounding up recipes and ideas from her friends and neighbors in York, Pennsylvania.

I would like to thank my sister Lelamay Morehead and her neighbors and friends in Morgan Hill, California, in the heart of zucchini country. They've kept me supplied with a wealth of handed-down, grassroots recipes and ideas, many of which you'll find in this book.

To Kay Bloss, my gratitude for her help in typing my recipes and manuscript, for taste-testing many of the dishes and for the valid comments she offered along the way.

As always, my husband, George Bateman, has been of tremendous help to me. He has eaten his way through another of my cookbooks and is still an enthusiastic eater and critic.

# Contents

# Introduction

This book is about all the colorful, exciting, delicious, light, fresh-tasting, inexpensive dishes you can make with zucchini and carrots. From low-cal, off-beat appetizers, through colorful soups and salads, to main dishes and unusual breads and desserts, carrot and zucchini recipes seem legion. The more I use them and the more I talk about them to neighbors, friends, and food associates, the more I find tempting ideas I'd like to try.

Like the elder brother of the prodigal son, zucchini and carrots are with us always—and, at an affordable price. Pristine asparagus has its brief, expensive glory in the spring. Fresh corn, tomatoes, and green beans taste sweetest and cost less when they've soaked up hours and days of hot summer sun. But the old reliables, zucchini and carrots, are always in our markets in top condition—zucchini, shiny green and gentle flavored; carrots, orangey gold, sweet, and crisp—both freshly harvested year round and begging to be used.

The analogy of the elder son ends, however, with saying that zucchini and carrots are always with us. They are unlike the elder son, who, I've always felt, was made to appear a sort of dull, dutiful clod. The Biblical writers make the prodigal son seem like a rather exciting fellow. In the dictionary sense, zucchini and carrots are truly the prodigal vegetables— yielding profusely, lavishly abundant. Generally, I'm afraid we don't appreciate their marvelous color and good flavors, their relatively low calorie count, their modest price, and their vital contribution to our good health. But you will appreciate them, I think, after you try some of the appealing recipes in this book.

In the first chapter, I've given numerous ways to cook zucchini and carrots with fresh appeal. They should not be boiled to death in gallons of water, but sautéed or stir-fried until crisply tender. Or steamed and puréed to velvety richness. Or baked with crunchy toppings. Or deep-fried into crisp, succulent sticks that will give those favorite French fries a run for the money.

Other chapters follow with equally exciting ideas: Hot and chilled soups; crisp raw salads; and continental mixtures of marinated, cooked vegetables. Among the omelets and soufflés, you will find many ideas borrowed from good Italian cooks who seem to put zucchini in everything. I've also worked out ways to use zucchini in traditional, often more expensive, eggplant dishes. Chefs and good cooks the world over have always used carrots for stocks and stews, and as bright accents for meats and casseroles and I've done the same.

There are surprising carrot and zucchini breads and muffins, moist and rich. And would you believe it, marvelous cakes, pies, cookies and puddings, often laced with spices and nuts, and moistly delicious to the last crumb.

The last chapter, Good Neighbor Recipe Exchange, is just that. It includes recipes I've collected from special neighbors and friends around the country since I started the book. The name of each contributor and her town are given so you can see how carrots and zucchini are favorites everywhere.

This is not intended as a vegetarian cookbook, nor as a natural foods cookbook. It does, however, stress the joys of good fresh food cooked simply and appealingly. I think our young families whose life-styles place value and emphasis on freshness and simplicity will like it. This book, I hope, will have interest for the more mature family cook who is constantly seeking new ways to brighten the year-in, year-out tedium of cooking.

All of the recipes have been adapted or developed, tested, and revised or updated when needed, in my own home kitchen. They also have been taste-tested by my family, friends, neighbors, and assorted guests. We liked them all and hope you will too.

*Ruth Conrad Bateman*

# 1

# Good Cooking Ways

Zucchini and carrots are delightful foods. They have delicious light flavors you can live with and not tire of. Their bright colors are appealing. They are low-calorie and good for you! To enjoy their maximum natural goodness, buy them at their freshest. Cook briefly and season lightly to accent but not overwhelm them. At all costs, avoid that long boil in a big pot of water which washes out their colors and flavors and takes all the zing out of them.

# How To Buy

Fortunately, carrots are never out of season and zucchini seldom are. The recipes in this book call for crisp, fresh carrots and zucchini. If you have the place and the time, grow them. They're among the easiest of all vegetables for a beginner to grow. There's nothing quite like a sweet young carrot pulled from the earth or a baby zucchini plucked and eaten raw—or quickly cooked and drizzled with a little butter.

Carrots with pretty green tops are sold by the bunch; carrots without tops are sold loose in packages. Bunch carrots are preferred for salads, raw relishes and quick cooking. Packaged carrots are cheaper and are perfect for soups, stews, stocks, cakes, muffins and the like. Tiny finger-size carrots, julienne sticks, and crinkle-cut slices, both fresh and frozen, are available in packages in most supermarkets. The freshest, sweetest carrots are slender, have vivid color and long rootlets, and are smooth and free of cracks and blemishes.

Zucchini are generally sold loose, by the pound. The best and freshest are firm-fleshed, crisp, glossy, and tender-skinned, with a tuft of stem and no wrinkles near the ends. The color is usually a deep green, often with faint stripes or specks of gold or grey.

# Food Value Notes

Carrots are an excellent source of Vitamin A and contain only about 20 calories per carrot. Roughly, that's 160 calories in a pound, which will serve 3 to 4 persons. Zucchini, also, are low in calories, containing about 35 calories per 1 cup, cooked. They're a good source of Vitamin C, especially when eaten raw, as many of the recipes suggest; a fair source of Vitamin A; and, important, for some diets, low in sodium. Both vegetables are sources of natural and vital food elements you won't find in a vitamin bottle.

# Good Cooking Ways

**Sautéed, butter-steamed,** and **oriental stir-fry** are similar ways to cook vegetables quickly and keep them bright and fresh tasting. With the exception of vegetables baked whole in the skin, vegetables cooked by these methods retain the most food value. Vital nutrients and flavors are locked in by the pre-seal of fat, the colors set, and harmful air sealed out. Brief cooking and a minimum of liquid help retain the food values. No rich sauce is needed later, yet they have the look and taste of a buttered vegetable.

**Sauté:** In all three methods, *slices, dices, shreds* or *strips* are cooked and stirred, in a little heated oil or butter in a heavy pan over high heat until the vegetables are shiny. Then, for the basic *sauté,* no liquid is added. The shiny vegetables are covered and cooked in their own juices at a lower heat until crisp-tender. It is essential to use very fresh, tender, young vegetables and to pay careful attention during the few minutes of cooking time. *Zucchini with Walnuts, The Four Seasons* and *Orange Zest Carrots* are good examples of basic sauté (see index for both).

**Butter-Steamed:** For *butter-steamed* vegetables, add a little hot stock or water to the sautéed vegetables. Cover pan and steam until vegetables are crisp-tender and just enough liquid remains to lightly sauce them. See *Zucchini* or *Carrot Celery Sauté* (index) for specific times and amounts.

**Oriental Stir-Fry:** Vegetables cooked the *oriental stir-fry* way are eaten with enthusiasm everywhere because of their natural fresh taste and appetizing appearance. Very hot oil in a heavy wide pan or a Chinese wok is used to stir-fry over very high heat. When colors are intensified and set and everything is shiny, a few spoonfuls of hot liquid are added. The pan is then covered and vegetables steamed until crisp-tender. Generally, the cooking liquid is seasoned and thickened with cornstarch. See *Zucchini Stir-Fry* (index) for specific details.

**Steamed:** This is the preferred way to cook vegetables you plan to stuff, bake, serve with a sauce, or put in a casserole. Use a heavy pan with a tight-fitting lid. Put in water, usually to a depth of ½ inch. The amount needed varies with the shape and weight of the pan, the freshness of the vegetables, etc. The point is, it is not necessary to drown vegetables in water to cook them. (Zucchini is a very watery vegetable. If cooked in lots of water, it becomes limp, soggy, tasteless, and uninteresting.) Heat water to boiling with or without salt (some cooks prefer to salt later), add vegetables, and cover pan. Lower heat and steam until tender. For purées, soups, and soufflés, cook vegetables until very tender, usually 25 to 30 minutes. More water and less salt is needed for carrots than for zucchini. A pinch of sugar seems to bring out the natural sweetness of carrots. Some purists prefer to steam vegetables on a rack or in a perforated steamer, *over* not *in* boiling water. This takes longer and is more suitable for zucchini than for carrots or other root vegetables.

# Cooking Pans

A heavy pan with a tight-fitting lid is absolutely essential for all these methods. Obviously you can not cook vegetables with little or no water unless you have suitable pans—of heavy, good quality material, with tight lids to prevent rapid evaporation of moisture and to allow vegetables to cook in their own juices.

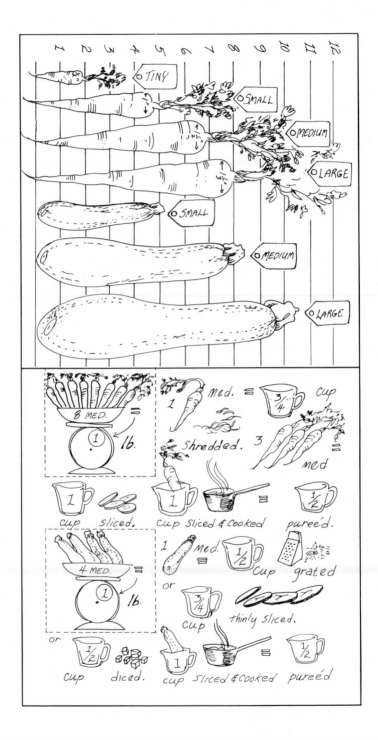

# Zucchini and Carrot Sizes and Measures

Ideas of vegetable sizes vary around the country. To help you shop for carrots and zucchini, these are the approximate sizes and amounts I used in working out the recipes for this book.

## Carrots

Tiny carrots—2 to 3 inches long, no more than ½ inch thick
Small carrots—3 to 5 inches long, up to 1 inch thick
Medium carrots—6 to 8 inches long, up to 1½ inches at crown
Large carrots—about 8 inches long, 1¾ inches at crown

6 to 8 medium carrots weigh about 1 pound
1 medium carrot makes about ¾ cup, coarsely grated or shredded
3 medium carrots make 1 cup, sliced
1 cup sliced carrot, cooked, makes about ½ cup puréed or sieved

## Zucchini

Small zucchini—4 to 5 inches long, about 1 inch thick
Medium zucchini—6 to 8 inches long, up to 1½ inches thick
Large zucchini—over 8 inches long, 1¾ to 2 inches thick
Giant zucchini—I never see them in my markets, but have them in my own garden when I don't pick the zucchini every day. They can become enormous almost overnight. If home-grown and fresh, I find large zucchini are still tender and good. If purchased at roadside stands where vegetables may not be first-day fresh, large zucchini are apt to be seedy and tough-skinned, less succulent, and lacking in flavor.

4-5 medium zucchini weigh about 1 pound.
1 medium zucchini makes about ½ cup, coarsely grated or shredded;
    ¾ to 1 cup, thinly sliced; or ½ cup diced.
1 cup sliced, cooked zucchini makes about ½ cup puréed.

# Zucchini with Walnuts,
# The Four Seasons

The Four Seasons Restaurant in New York serves vegetables imaginatively and beautifully. This is a favorite zucchini dish and a delightful combination of flavors.

6 servings

*6 medium (6 inches long) zucchini, unpeeled*
*1 cup walnut halves*
*2 tablespoons butter*
*Salt and freshly ground black pepper*

Wash and trim zucchini and cut into slices 1/8 inch thick. Reserve 8 walnut halves for garnish and coarsely chop the rest. Melt butter in heavy saucepan, add zucchini, and sauté, stirring gently and constantly until almost tender, 3 to 5 minutes. Add chopped walnuts, salt and pepper to taste. Cook gently, stirring until zucchini is crisply tender. Garnish with the walnut halves.

# Shredded Zucchini Sauté

This dish is simple but fresh and delicious with a slightly crunchy texture.

4 servings

*8 medium, tender young zucchini, unpeeled*
*2 tablespoons olive or vegetable oil*
*1 to 2 cloves garlic, finely chopped*
*Fresh lemon juice*
*Salt*
*Chopped parsley*

Remove tips from the zucchini and shred coarsely. You should have about 4 cups. Heat oil in heavy saucepan and drop in zucchini and garlic. Stir-fry over low heat until zucchini is coated with oil. Cover and cook, shaking pan and stirring zucchini frequently, until tender but still a bit crunchy, 3 to 5 minutes. Season with fresh lemon juice and salt to taste, and a spoonful of chopped parsley. Serve at once.

# Zucchini Bacon Sauté

Here is a favorite flavor combination—zucchini, bacon, onion and tomato. It may be served as a side dish or as a luncheon entrée.

4 servings

*3 to 4 medium zucchini, unpeeled*
*3 slices bacon, diced*
*1 onion, chopped*
*½ teaspoon salt*
*Freshly ground black pepper*
*½ teaspoon dried oregano, crumbled*
*1 medium tomato, peeled and diced*

Scrub zucchini, remove tips, and cut on the diagonal into longish ovals about ¼ inch thick. Fry bacon crisp in heavy saucepan; drain on paper towels. In 2 tablespoons of the drippings (or use margarine if you prefer) cook onion a few minutes, until soft. Add zucchini, cook and stir until slices are well coated with fat. Add bacon bits, seasonings and tomato. Cover and cook gently until crisp-tender, 4 to 6 minutes, shaking pan often to prevent sticking.

# Zucchini with Fennel

Quickly sautéed zucchini accented with garlic and fennel.

4 servings

4 medium zucchini (about 1 pound), unpeeled
2 tablespoons olive or other oil
1 clove garlic, minced
½ teaspoon salt
½ teaspoon sugar
½ teaspoon fennel seeds
2 teaspoons red wine vinegar

Scrub zucchini, remove tips, and cut into ¼ inch slices. Heat oil in heavy saucepan or skillet. Add zucchini and sauté over moderate heat until shiny and well coated with oil. Add remaining ingredients, stir well and cover. Cook gently until tender, 4 to 5 minutes.

SEE ALSO *Sautéed Zucchini, Vermouth* (p. 168)
*Zucchini Fritti* (p. 168)

11

# Zucchini Steam Sauté

An appealing example of a quick, nutritious, butter-steamed vegetable. Olive oil is used in place of butter, with green onions, both delicious accents for gentle-flavored zucchini.

4 servings

*8 small zucchini (4 to 5 inches long)*
*2 green onions*
*1 tablespoon olive or vegetable oil*
*2 to 4 tablespoons boiling water or chicken broth*
*½ teaspoon salt*
*Freshly ground black pepper*

Wash and trim zucchini but do not peel. Slice on a diagonal into ovals. Slice green onions and tops. Heat oil in heavy pan with a tight lid and add onions and zucchini. Stir with wooden spoon over medium-high heat until colors deepen and vegetables are shiny. Add boiling water or chicken broth and salt. Cover and cook over lowered heat until crisp-tender, 4 to 5 minutes. Add a few grindings of pepper and serve.

# Elena's Colache

Since Indian days, squash and corn have been a popular vegetable combination. Fresh tomatoes add extra flavor and color.

6 servings

4 or 5 medium zucchini (1 pound)
4 ears fresh corn (or 2 cups canned
   or frozen whole kernel corn)
3 fresh tomatoes
1 small onion, finely chopped
¼ cup butter or margarine
Salt and freshly ground black pepper
Sugar

Scrub unpeeled zucchini, trim off tips, halve lengthwise, then slice. Cut kernels from ears of corn. Halve tomatoes, press lightly to push out seeds, then cube tomatoes. In heavy saucepan, cook onion in melted butter until soft, 3 to 5 minutes. Add vegetables and stir until all are well-coated with butter. Season with salt and pepper and a pinch of sugar. Cover and cook slowly until tender, about 15 minutes. Shake pan frequently to prevent sticking.

# Zucchini in Sour Cream

I made this recipe for my first book, *I Love To Cook Book* published by Ward Ritchie Press. It has remained a favorite with my family and guests. Vary the herb seasonings as you wish.

4 servings

2 pounds medium zucchini, unpeeled
1 tablespoon butter or margarine
2 minced green onions
2 to 4 tablespoons boiling water
½ teaspoon salt, or to taste
⅓ cup sour cream
1 tablespoon chopped fresh dill,
 (or 1 teaspoon dried)

Trim zucchini and cut into halves crosswise then lengthwise. Cut into slender julienne sticks. Heat butter or margarine in heavy saucepan with tight lid. Toss in onion and zucchini and stir with wooden spoon until shiny and well coated with fat. Add boiling water and salt. Cover tightly and steam gently 4 to 5 minutes. Moisture should be practically evaporated, zucchini crisply tender. If not, leave uncovered a few seconds. Stir in sour cream and fresh or dried dill. Cover pan and heat a few seconds to blend flavors.

## VARIATIONS

Caraway seeds, crumbled sweet basil or fennel seeds may be used in place of dill.

# Sweet Creamy Zucchini

This is French in flavor rather than Middle or East European as is the preceding recipe. Sweet cream, tarragon and basil are the gentle seasonings used.

4 servings

4 tender young zucchini
2 tablespoons butter or margarine
2 minced green onions or
   1 tablespoon minced shallots
½ teaspoon salt
Generous pinch of dried tarragon leaves
Generous pinch of dried basil leaves
⅓ cup heavy cream
Freshly ground black pepper

Remove tips from unpeeled zucchini and halve each lengthwise. Slice thinly or cut into slender sticks. Melt butter in heavy saucepan and add zucchini and green onions or shallots. Stir over moderate heat until zucchini is shiny and well coated with butter and the onions softened, about 3 to 4 minutes. Sprinkle with salt, tarragon, and basil to your liking (use fresh herbs if you have them). Pour in cream, stir gently, and cover pan. Lower heat and cook slowly until zucchini is tender-crisp and has absorbed most of the cream, 5 to 8 minutes. Raise lid occasionally and shake pan gently to baste zucchini with cream. Season lightly with a little freshly ground pepper.

# Zucchini Stir-Fry

Lightly cooked the Chinese way with bits of bacon and soy sauce.

4 servings

2 slices bacon, diced
1 green onion, sliced
3 medium zucchini, sliced diagonally
½ cup chicken broth
1 teaspoon cornstarch
1 teaspoon soy sauce
½ teaspoon salt
2 teaspoons cold water

Cook bacon until crisp in heavy saucepan or skillet. Drain on paper towels. To 2 tablespoons drippings, add onion and zucchini. Stir-fry until vegetables are shiny. Pour in chicken broth, cover pan, and steam vegetables 3 to 5 minutes. Blend remaining ingredients and stir into broth. Stir and heat to boiling. Turn into serving dish and top with bacon bits.

# Mediterranean Zucchini
# and Mushrooms

Bright parsley, garlic and olive oil perfume this lively dish that can be cooked in minutes.

4 servings

4 to 5 medium zucchini (1 pound), unpeeled
Salt
¼ pound fresh mushrooms
1 large clove garlic, minced
½ cup finely chopped green onions
¼ cup minced parsley
2 tablespoons olive oil
2 tablespoons butter or margarine
2 tablespoons fresh lemon juice
Freshly ground black pepper

Wash zucchini, remove tips, and cut into diagonal slices about ½-inch thick. Spread on paper towels and sprinkle lightly with salt. Let stand 30 minutes and blot up excess moisture. Rinse mushrooms, pat dry with paper towels, and cut in halves. Prepare garlic, onions and parsley. Heat oil in large heavy skillet. Add garlic and cook a few seconds. Toss in zucchini and onions. Stir over medium-high heat until all slices are shiny with oil and beginning to cook. Cover and cook gently 3 to 4 minutes. Push zucchini to side of pan and add butter. When the butter is hot, add mushrooms and stir until coated with butter. Sprinkle lightly with salt, half the lemon juice and parsley. Stir well, cover and cook gently 3 to 4 minutes. Sprinkle with rest of the lemon juice and pepper. Serve hot as a side dish or a light entree, with chunks of French Bread.

SEE ALSO Ratatouille (p. 114)

17

# Baked Zucchini Parmesan

This is an easy make-ahead dish ideal for buffets or parties.

4 to 6 servings

*6 to 7 medium zucchini (1½ pounds), unpeeled*
*½ cup boiling water*
*Salt and freshly ground black pepper*
*3 tablespoons olive oil or melted butter*
*6 tablespoons grated Parmesan cheese*

Wash zucchini and remove tips. Drop into a heavy saucepan with about ½ cup boiling water and ½ teaspoon salt. Cover pan tightly and steam zucchini until crisp-tender, about 10 minutes. Drain and split lengthwise. Lay in a shallow baking dish, one layer deep. Sprinkle with salt and pepper and a dash of your favorite herb, if you like. Drizzle with oil or melted butter, and sprinkle with Parmesan. Bake in moderately hot oven (375°F.) about 20 minutes.

# Crisp Baked Zucchini

The crisp golden coating of cracker crumbs and Parmesan cheese are delicious accents to the gentle flavor of zucchini.

3 to 4 servings

*4 to 5 medium zucchini (1 pound), unpeeled*
*Salt*
*½ cup finely crushed saltine crackers*
*½ cup grated Parmesan cheese*
*½ cup mayonnaise*

Scrub zucchini, remove tips, and cut lengthwise into flat slices about ¼ inch thick. Place in sieve or colander and sprinkle with salt. Let stand 15 to 20 minutes. Blot off moisture with paper towels. Combine cracker crumbs and cheese in flat pan. Spread zucchini slices on each side with thin layer of mayonnaise and drop into crumbs to coat evenly. Lay rather close together on greased cookie sheet or jellyroll pan. Bake at 400°F. until crisply golden, about 15 to 20 minutes.

SEE ALSO *Ham Stuffed Zucchini* (p. 70)
  *Cheese Stuffed Zucchini* (p. 72)

# Zucchini Potato Purée

Pretty flecks of green zucchini and onion are delicious and different in these airy whipped potatoes—especially good with grilled lamb or chicken.

6 servings

2 pounds russet potatoes, peeled and cut in chunks
1 teaspoon salt
1 cup boiling water
¼ cup butter or margarine
2 medium zucchini, diced
6 green onions and parts of tops, sliced
1½ cups milk
Freshly ground black pepper

Cook potatoes in boiling salted water, in covered saucepan, until tender, about 20 minutes. When they are almost done, combine butter, zucchini, onions and milk and simmer gently until tender, 5 to 10 minutes. Drain potatoes, if necessary, and shake pan over low heat to dry potatoes (this makes them fluffier). Beat potatoes with small electric hand beater, while still over low heat if possible (or beat in electric mixer). Gradually beat in zucchini mixture. Keep beating until potatoes are very light and fluffy and the zucchini and onions are practically absorbed. Add more hot milk, if needed. Taste and season with salt and pepper as needed. Serve very hot.

# Broiled Zucchini Sticks

Make these crisp golden sticks to accompany any of your grilled meats, particularly chicken, lamb or steaks. They're pretty, taste light, and are snap-easy to make. They also make a nice change-of-pace appetizer to serve with drinks.

4 servings

*4 to 5 medium zucchini (about 1 pound), unpeeled*
*3 to 4 tablespoons melted butter or margarine*
*Salt, seasoned salt, or garlic salt*
*½ cup freshly grated Parmesan cheese*

Remove tips, halve zucchini crosswise, and cut each half in quarters lengthwise. Dip in melted butter, season lightly with plain salt or one of the seasoned salts, then coat with Parmesan. Place on cookie sheet and broil 4 to 6 inches from heat until golden crisp, about 6 minutes.

# Zucchini Cheese Pancakes

Call them pancakes or pan-fried fritters, they have a delicate flavor and an appealing texture. As an unusual idea for breakfast, serve with crisp bacon or ham and your favorite eggs.

12 to 15 small pancakes

2 medium unpeeled zucchini, shredded or coarsely grated
½ teaspoon salt
2 ounces cream cheese (¼ cup)
¼ cup freshly grated Parmesan cheese
2 tablespoons flour
1 teaspoon grated onion
Black pepper to taste
2 eggs, beaten
Oil, margarine, or butter for frying

Spread zucchini on foil and sprinkle with salt. Let stand 1 hour and press out moisture. In small mixing bowl, soften cream cheese and blend in Parmesan. Stir in zucchini, flour, grated onion, pepper to taste and beaten eggs. Heat a film of light vegetable oil (or a mixture of oil and margarine or butter) in heavy skillet. Drop mixture by tablespoons into hot oil and cook until browned on each side, just a few minutes. Serve hot.

# Fabulous Zucchini French Fries

Pass around a basket of these with cool drinks at your next party as do many restaurants nowadays. Zucchini fries are crisp and light, with a fresh new fantastic flavor. I've also served these alongside potato french fries with steaks and hamburgers. The zucchini fries disappeared twice as fast.

4 to 5 servings

*4 medium zucchini*
*Flour for zucchini*
*Salt*
*1 cup flour*
*2 eggs*
*1½ tablespoons water*
*1 cup grated Parmesan cheese*
*Seasoned salt or garlic salt [optional]*
*Vegetable oil for deep-frying*

Remove tips from unpeeled zucchini and cut into shoestring strips 3 or 4 inches long. Sprinkle well with salt and roll lightly in flour. Shake off excess flour and drop strips, a handful at a time, into eggs beaten lightly with 1½ tablespoons water. In wide shallow pan, combine flour with Parmesan cheese and seasoned salt or garlic salt, if you wish. Roll zucchini in flour mixture to coat evenly and spread on paper towels to dry. This may be done ahead of the time you wish to fry the zucchini. Heat vegetable oil to 375°F. in deep kettle. Fry strips, a handful at a time, until crisp and golden. Drain on paper towels set in shallow tray. Keep strips warm in 250°F. oven until all are fried. Heap into a napkin-lined basket and sprinkle again with salt.

SEE ALSO *Fritto Misto* (p. 48)

23

# Perino's Zucchini Florentine

Directions for these crisp fried zucchini sticks were given to me by the elegant Mr. Alex Perino himself. He suggested the two-step frying so the zucchini sticks can be done ahead. You may prepare them all in one operation, if you prefer.

4 to 5 servings

4 to 5 medium zucchini (6 inches long), unpeeled
Milk
Flour
2 eggs
2 cups fine dry bread crumbs (from French
    or Italian bread), sifted
Oil for deep fat frying
Salt

Trim ends from zucchini and cut into thin julienne strips. Dip in milk then into flour. Shake off the excess flour and dip into eggs beaten with 2 tablespoons milk. Dip sticks into fine dry bread crumbs. Roll zucchini in crumbs to coat evenly and place on paper towels or a wire rack to dry. Blanch or precook in deep, hot cooking oil heated to 375°F. until pale gold in color. (Corn or peanut oil is preferred by Perino's.) At serving time, again drop into the hot oil and cook until crisp and golden brown. Sprinkle with salt and serve at once.

# Squash Blossom Fritters

For this delicacy, if you have a garden and grow zucchini, gather large male blossoms (they have no tiny squash behind them) early in the morning. Otherwise, look for squash flowers in Italian or Mexican markets.

12 fritters

*Beer Fritter Batter*
*12 large zucchini blossoms*
*Vegetable oil for frying*
*Salt*

Make *Beer Fritter Batter* at least 1 hour ahead. Rinse blossoms gently and dry in a soft towel. Heat oil in deep kettle to 375°F. Dip flowers, one at a time, into batter and fry in hot oil until golden. Drain on paper towels and sprinkle with salt. Serve hot as an unusual appetizer or vegetable garnish.

## Beer Fritter Batter

*1 egg*
*1 tablespoon oil or melted butter*
*½ cup flour*
*¼ teaspoon salt*
*½ cup flat beer*
*1 extra egg white*

Beat egg with oil and stir in flour mixed with salt. Add beer and stir only until batter is mixed. Let stand 1 to 2 hours. When you are ready to use batter, beat extra egg white until stiff and lightly fold it in.

# Orange Zest Carrots

The original recipe called these "panned carrots," an old-fashioned term we seldom use nowadays. These are shredded young carrots tossed with a little butter and orange zest then steamed in their own liquid. A flavorful and nutritious way to cook carrots.

4 servings

6 to 8 young, tender carrots
3 to 4 green onions and 2 inches of tops
3 tablespoons butter or margarine
1 tablespoon shredded orange peel
½ teaspoon sugar
½ teaspoon salt

Scrape carrots lightly and shred on coarse side of grater. Chop onions and cook gently without browning in heavy saucepan in the melted butter. When onions are soft, stir in carrots, orange peel, sugar and salt. Stir until everything is shiny with butter. Cover pan tightly and cook over very low heat until carrots are crisply tender, 5 to 8 minutes. Shake pan frequently to keep carrots from sticking.

# Shredded Carrots and Onions

The crunchy bacon topping is optional—or you can substitute soy "bacon" bits.

4 servings

8 to 10 young, medium carrots
1 onion
2 strips bacon, diced
3 tablespoons butter or margarine
Salt and freshly ground black pepper

Scrape and shred carrots. You should have 3 cups, shredded. Chop onion finely. Cook bacon crisp and drain on paper towels. Heat butter or margarine (or part bacon drippings) in heavy saucepan or skillet. Stir in carrots and onion and season well with salt and pepper. Cover and cook until crisply tender, 5 to 8 minutes, shaking pan often or stirring to prevent sticking. Sprinkle top with bacon bits and serve pronto.

# Oven Shredded Carrots

With an oven meal, put shredded carrots and onions described above in baking dish. Season with salt, pepper and butter or margarine and cover tightly. Bake at 350°F. for about 30 minutes. Sprinkle with bacon bits, if desired.

# Carrot Celery Sauté

The crunchy crisp texture and bright colors of these two vegetables are pleasing and tasty. Cooked this way they need no extra seasonings.

6 servings

4 to 5 medium-small young carrots
4 stalks green celery
1 tablespoon light vegetable oil
⅓ cup boiling water or chicken broth
½ teaspoon salt
¼ teaspoon sugar

Scrape carrots lightly and cut on a slant into thin, oval slices about ¼-inch thick. Peel any tough strings from celery and cut on a slant into thin slices. This is easy if vegetables are laid out on a cutting board and sliced with a heavy, sharp chef's or cook's knife. Heat oil in heavy saucepan. Add celery and carrots and sauté over high heat, stirring constantly, until vegetables are shiny with oil. Add boiling water or broth, salt and sugar. Cover tightly. When water boils again, reduce heat and simmer until vegetables are crisp-tender, 7 to 10 minutes. Serve at once.

### VARIATION

Dice and fry 2 or 3 slices of bacon until crisp. Crumble over cooked *Carrot Celery Sauté, Zucchini Steam Sauté, Carrot Steam Sauté* (see index) just before serving.

# Orange Carrots

4 servings

*6 to 8 medium carrots (about 1 pound)*
*½ teaspoon salt*
*Pinch of sugar*
*¾ cup boiling water*
*2 tablespoons butter or margarine*
*½ teaspoon grated fresh orange peel*
*1 tablespoon chopped green onion*
*1 orange, peeled and cut in bite-size pieces*

Scrape carrots and cut into ½-inch slices. Cook covered in boiling water with salt and sugar until just tender, 10 to 15 minutes. Drain and push to side of pan. Add butter and heat until melted. Toss carrots until they are well coated and shiny. Add rest of ingredients and stir over low heat until heated through.

# Mixed Vegetable Stir-Fry

You can use an infinite variety of vegetables for this dish. Try for contrast of flavors, colors, and textures.

4 to 5 servings.

8 to 10 small, young carrots scraped,
    sliced in ¼-inch diagonals
2 stalks green celery, sliced in ¼-inch diagonals
2 to 3 small unpeeled zucchini,
    sliced in ¼-inch diagonals
3 to 4 green onions, cut into 1-inch pieces
½ green pepper, halved, seeded, cut in strips
Peanut or vegetable oil
1 clove garlic, split
Salt
Soy sauce
2 tablespoons thinly sliced, natural skin almonds, toasted

🐚 Have all vegetables ready before you start cooking. Heat oil with garlic in large heavy skillet, until very hot. Remove garlic. Add carrots and celery and stir-fry until shiny with oil and partly cooked, 3 to 4 minutes. Add zucchini, green onions, and pepper strips and salt to taste. Continue to stir-fry 2 to 4 minutes longer, until vegetables are tender but still crisp. Sprinkle with a dash of soy sauce and the almonds. Serve at once.

# Lemon Dill Carrots

4 servings

12 medium-small young carrots
3 tablespoons butter or margarine
½ teaspoon salt
¼ teaspoon sugar
2 tablespoons water
1 tablespoon chopped fresh dill (or 1 teaspoon dried)
Lemon juice

Scrape carrots and cut into thin julienne strips. Melt butter or margarine in heavy saucepan and add carrot strips. Stir to coat evenly with butter then sprinkle with salt, sugar and water. Cover tightly and cook over moderately low heat, shaking pan often, until carrots are tender-crisp, 4 to 8 minutes. All moisture should be evaporated by then. Stir in dill and lemon juice to taste—about 2 teaspoons or more. Serve at once.

# Carrots Russe

Cook carrots as described in *Lemon Dill Carrots*. When they are tender-crisp, turn into a warm bowl and top with ½ cup sour cream seasoned lightly with chopped chives, dill and lemon juice.

# Lemon Glazed Carrots

1 bunch tender young carrots                                   4 servings
  (about 1½ pounds)
Water
Salt
Sugar
2 tablespoons butter or margarine
2 tablespoons fresh lemon juice
Chopped parsley


Scrape carrots and cut into thin slices. Cook in heavy saucepan in ½ inch boiling water with a pinch each of salt and sugar until just tender, about 5 to 8 minutes. Drain if necessary or uncover last few minutes to evaporate liquid. In same pan melt butter or margarine and add 2 tablespoons sugar and lemon juice. Simmer until sugar is dissolved. Add carrots and cook gently, stirring frequently until carrots are well glazed.


# Lemon Honey Carrots

1 bunch of tiny carrots (about 1½ pounds,                     4 servings
  3 inches long)
Water
Salt
3 tablespoons melted butter or margarine
3 tablespoons honey
1½ teaspoons grated fresh orange peel
1½ teaspoons grated fresh lemon peel
1 teaspoon fresh lemon juice

Scrape carrots lightly and cook, covered, in ½ inch boiling water with ½ teaspoon salt. Cook until crisp-tender, about 10 to 12 minutes. Drain and push to side of pan. Add butter, honey, peels and juice. Stir over very low heat until carrots are glazed, about 5 minutes.

# Carrots Amandine

This smacks of the Belgian way with carrots—enriched with cream and lightly sweetened with brown sugar.

4 servings

*1½ pounds small carrots (or longer slender carrots*
*    cut in 3-inch pieces)*
*1 cup water*
*½ teaspoon salt*
*½ teaspoon sugar*
*White pepper*
*½ teaspoon ground ginger*
*2 tablespoons brown sugar*
*½ cup heavy cream*
*2 tablespoons thinly sliced natural skin almonds, toasted*

Scrape carrots and cut longer, slender carrots into 3-inch pieces and split lengthwise. Put in heavy saucepan with water, salt and sugar. Cover and cook until nearly tender, about 10 minutes. Drain, if necessary, or uncover last few minutes to evaporate liquid. Sprinkle with a little white pepper, ginger and brown sugar. Pour in heavy cream and cook over low heat until cream thickens slightly and about half of it has cooked into carrots. Shake pan often and turn carrots with a wooden spoon to coat evenly with sauce. Turn into a warm serving bowl and sprinkle with almonds.

# French Glazed Carrots

A marvelous flavor results when carrots are cooked very, very slowly, with seasonings in the cooking water, until all liquid has evaporated. Try it.

4 servings

1 bunch (about 1½ pounds) tiny carrots
¼ cup unsalted butter
2 tablespoons sugar
1 teaspoon salt
1½ cups water
1 tablespoon minced fresh parsley

Scrape carrots and cut into 3-inch lengths, if they're longer. Don't use larger, heavier, mature carrots. Melt butter in heavy saucepan and add carrots. Stir until coated, then add sugar, salt and water. Heat to boiling, then lower heat and simmer carrots uncovered until tender, liquid has evaporated, and carrots are glazed, 15 to 20 minutes. Shake pan frequently to keep carrots from sticking. Takes a bit of watching and a sense of timing to know when they're ready—but the flavor is worth it. Sprinkle with parsley.

# Carrots Vichy

A favorite French way to cook carrots that appears in many cookbooks in several guises. Simply cook carrots slowly in water (bottled Vichy water if you want to be authentic) with butter until tender.

*10 to 12 tender young carrots*          4 to 5 servings
*Water*
*½ teaspoon salt*
*½ teaspoon sugar*
*2 tablespoons butter or margarine*
*White or black pepper*
*1 tablespoon minced fresh parsley*

Scrape carrots and cut in slices or sticks. Put in heavy saucepan with about 1 cup water, salt, sugar, and butter or margarine. Cover and cook over very low heat until carrots are tender and liquid has evaporated, 20 to 30 minutes. Lift lid occasionally and shake pan. Season lightly with white or black pepper, additional salt if needed, and sprinkle with parsley.

# Carrots with Mint Butter

*2 cups sliced or julienne carrots (6 to 8 carrots)*          3 servings
*Water*
*½ teaspoon salt*
*½ teaspoon sugar*
*2 tablespoons butter or margarine*
*2 tablespoons chopped fresh mint leaves*
    *or 2 teaspoons dried mint*

Put carrots in heavy saucepan with ½ inch boiling water, salt and sugar. Cover and cook until crisp tender. Drain if necessary or uncover last few minutes to evaporate liquid. Add butter to pan, stir over low heat until butter melts, then add chopped mint. Stir and serve at once.

# Creamy Carrots and Turnips

The flavors of young carrots and turnips, seasoned with nutmeg and cream make a delicious combination—especially good with lamb or roast pork.

4 servings

6 medium carrots, scraped
4 to 5 small young turnips, peeled
Salt
Sugar
2 tablespoons unsalted butter or margarine
¼ cup heavy cream
Pinch of nutmeg
White pepper
Minced parsley

Cut carrots into 3-inch lengths, then into julienne sticks. Slice turnips rather thinly and cut into julienne sticks. You should have about 2 cups each. Put into heavy saucepan with 1 inch of boiling water. Add ½ teaspoon salt and ½ teaspoon sugar. Cover pan and cook gently until vegetables are tender, about 10 minutes. Uncover for the last few minutes, if liquid has not evaporated. Add butter and cream, and season lightly with nutmeg and white pepper. Leave pan over very low heat, uncovered, stirring and shaking often until at least half the cream sauce has cooked into the vegetables. Sprinkle with minced parsley just before serving.

# Carrot Purée, Le St. Germain

Bright flowers in window boxes and lacy curtains at the windows are traditional French at the chic, small Los Angeles restaurant, Le St. Germain. So are these creamy light puréed carrots. They are fabulous and very popular.

4 servings

8 medium, young carrots
¾ cup boiling water
Salt
¼ teaspoon sugar
2 tablespoons soft, unsalted butter
2 to 4 tablespoons heavy cream
White pepper
Nutmeg

Trim and scrape carrots. Halve or quarter and cook covered in boiling water with ¼ teaspoon each salt and sugar. Cook until tender enough to mash, 10 to 15 minutes. Drain if necessary or uncover last few minutes to evaporate liquid. Whip with electric mixer, rotary beater or whisk, still over low heat if possible, to a smooth creamy purée. Beat in unsalted butter and 2 to 4 tablespoons heavy cream, or enough to make purée light and creamy. Season with a little more salt if needed, white pepper and a dash of nutmeg. Serve very hot.

# Carrot Potato Purée

Use this persuasive dish to get your non-carrot fanciers to eat them. It has a pretty color as well as delicious flavor.

6 servings

*1 pound slender young carrots, scraped*
*Salt*
*½ teaspoon sugar*
*1 pound medium russet potatoes, peeled*
*1 cup half-and-half*
*¼ cup butter*
*Generous pinch of nutmeg*
*Freshly ground black pepper*
*Minced parsley*

Cut carrots in halves or quarters. Cook, tightly covered, in 1 inch of boiling water with ¼ teaspoon salt and the sugar, until very tender, about 15 minutes. Cut potatoes in uniform pieces and cook same as carrots with ½ teaspoon salt (no sugar) until tender. Drain vegetables if necessary and return potatoes to low heat a few seconds to dry out. Mash together, and while still over very low heat beat until smooth, using a wooden spoon, potato masher or electric beater. Heat half-and-half and beat in along with the butter. Season with additional salt, if needed, add a pinch of nutmeg and pepper to taste. Whip until very light and fluffy. Heap into a warm bowl and sprinkle with parsley.

### VARIATIONS

**Cheese Top Golden Purée:** This recipe is not only a taste pleaser, but can be prepared well ahead of serving time.

Make *Carrot Potato Purée* as directed above and beat in 1 whole egg and 1 tablespoon minced parsley. Mound in flame proof dish and sprinkle with ½ cup grated sharp cheddar cheese. Heat at 400°F. a few minutes, then run under boiler to glaze cheese and fleck with brown.

38

# 2

# Lively Appetizers
and Soups

# Crudités

One of the nicest kinds of appetizers, and growing in popularity is this one of raw vegetables. Choose the freshest, prettiest vegetables and keep them natural looking and crisp. Arranged artfully in a basket, with salt and dips nearby, they look like a still-life painting. To insure crispness, bank a shallow bowl with chipped ice and set it in a suitable basket. Keeping a contrast of colors and shapes, nest vegetables in ice. Use whatever is available in the markets.

## A Popular Selection:

*Crisp raw carrots*
*Tender young zucchini*
*Radishes with leaves on top*
*Cherry tomatoes*
*Celery, young turnips or cucumbers (all or one of these)*
*Cauliflowerets or broccoli flowerets*
*Green and red bell pepper strips*
*Fennel (called finnochio or sweet anise in some markets)*
*Coarse salt, seasoned salt or dips*

Crisp raw carrots may be cut in julienne sticks or sliced on a slant into longish ovals. The ovals are pretty and make excellent dippers for dunks with drinks. Home gardeners were the first to discover how good tender young raw zucchini tastes as an appetizer. Now the idea has caught on with others. Do them unpeeled in julienne sticks or sliced on a slant into ovals. Radishes and cherry tomatoes, both with a tuft of leaves left on, provide color and flavor contrast with celery, turnip or cucumber sticks or slices. Thinly sliced cauliflower and broccoli flowerets are popular and so are bright green and red bell pepper strips. Fennel makes an unusual addition to the crudités assortment. Cut off green top and any tough outer layers of the white bulb. Slice white bulb thinly. Pack everything separately in plastic bags with ice cubes and refrigerate so they'll be dewy-fresh and crisp when you serve them.

Offer a seasoned salt, coarse kosher or sea salt for the dieters or those who don't care for dips. Fresh olive oil mayonnaise, often laced with plenty of garlic, is a favorite French sauce for crudités. Here are other suggestions for easy sauces that are good with raw vegetables:

# Garlic Tarragon Mayonnaise

1 cup

*1 clove garlic*
*¼ teaspoon salt*
*½ cup mayonnaise*
*½ cup sour cream*
*1½ tablespoons Dijon-type mustard*
*2 teaspoons dried tarragon leaves, crumbled*
*Lemon juice*

Crush garlic into salt and blend into mayonnaise. Stir in sour cream, mustard, and tarragon leaves. Mix well and add a few drops lemon juice. Taste and add additional salt if needed. Cover and refrigerate several hours to blend flavors.

### VARIATION

**Yogurt Tarragon Mayonnaise:** Combine equal parts unflavored yogurt and mayonnaise. Season same as in *Garlic Tarragon Mayonnaise.*

42

# Dill Dip

1½ cups

*½ cup sour cream*
*½ cup unflavored yogurt*
*½ cup mayonnaise*
*1 to 2 tablespoons minced green onion*
*2 tablespoons chopped fresh or 1 tablespoon dried dill*
*Salt*

Combine sour cream, yogurt and mayonnaise with green onion, dill and salt to taste. Cover and refrigerate to blend flavors.

# Anchovy Cheese Dip

2 cups

*1 package (8 ounces) cream cheese*
*½ cup sour cream*
*½ cup mayonnaise*
*1 tablespoon anchovy paste or 3 or 4 minced anchovies*
*1 clove garlic*
*Salt*

Combine cream cheese with sour cream, mayonnaise, anchovy paste. Beat until smooth and well blended. Crush to a paste a clove of garlic in a little salt and add it to the sauce. Mix well, cover and refrigerate several hours.

# Caponata

A colorful cold mixture of cooked eggplant, zucchini, peppers and other fresh vegetables, served as an antipasto all over Italy, but especially in Sicily. Keep a batch in the refrigerator for a refreshing appetizer or snack with crusty bread and wine or a drink.

6 servings

1 unpeeled eggplant, cut in 1-inch chunks
2 onions, thinly sliced
1 green pepper, seeded, cut in strips
3 medium zucchini, halved lengthwise, sliced
1 can (2 cups) Italian, pear-shaped tomatoes
6 to 8 tablespoons olive oil
  (part may be vegetable oil)
2 cloves garlic, chopped
1 teaspoon salt, or to taste
Freshly ground black pepper
2 tablespoons bottled capers and juice
1 dozen black Italian olives, chopped or whole
2 tablespoons chopped parsley
1 tablespoon sugar
2 to 3 tablespoons red wine vinegar, or to taste
Fresh lemon juice

Prepare vegetables and force tomatoes through a sieve. In large heavy pan, heat 2 tablespoons of the oil, add eggplant, and cook until it is soft and lightly browned. Remove to bowl. Heat more oil, add onions and peppers, stir until coated and shiny, and cook gently about 5 minutes.

Heat more oil, add the zucchini and garlic, stir until mixed with the oil, then cook gently 2 or 3 minutes longer. Add tomatoes, the browned eggplant, and salt and pepper to taste. Cook gently, stirring frequently, until vegetables are tender and liquid has cooked down somewhat, about 20 minutes. Add capers, olives and parsley. Mix sugar and vinegar, add to mixture, and taste it. Adjust seasonings if necessary. Cover and simmer 15 to 20 minutes longer, until flavors are richly blended. Cool caponata, then cover and refrigerate. This dish is even better the second day or the third. Remove from refrigerator 10 minutes before serving and splash with fresh lemon juice.

# Zucchini Curry Dip

This is a great low-cal, fresh-tasting dip, a favorite of dieters and nondieters. Adjust the amount of curry to your own taste.

2 cups

1½ cups shredded, unpeeled zucchini (about 2 medium)
1 cup unflavored yogurt
¼ cup mayonnaise
1½ tablespoons grated onion
Garlic salt or plain salt to taste
1 teaspoon curry powder

Shred enough tender young zucchini to make 1½ cups. Put into a strainer and press out excess moisture. You should end up with 1 cup of pressed zucchini. Combine with remaining ingredients. Cover and chill several hours to mellow flavors. Serve with chips or vegetable sticks.

# Broiled Zucchini Puffs

Here is a sizzling hot appetizer you can make in minutes. Grated raw zucchini in the topping is a pleasant surprise.

16 appetizers

*1 small young zucchini*
*½ cup mayonnaise*
*1½ tablespoons grated onion*
*2 long French rolls (about 8 inches)*
*1 cup grated Swiss cheese*

Grate unpeeled zucchini into sieve and press out the excess moisture. (You should have about ¼ cup). Stir into mayonnaise with grated onion. Cut each French roll into about 8 slices, 1 inch thick, and spread thickly with mayonnaise mixture. Sprinkle each with cheese and set on cookie sheet. Broil until puffed and golden, 3 to 5 minutes.

## VARIATION

**Chile Puffs:** Make mayonnaise topping for *Broiled Zucchini Puffs* and add finely diced, canned green chiles to taste—1 to 2 tablespoons. Spread on sliced rolls and sprinkle with mixture of grated cheddar and Parmesan cheese. Broil until puffed and golden.

# Antipasto Zucchini

Marinated zucchini or carrots—alone or in combination—add zest to an antipasto assortment of fresh raw vegetables, olives, pickled peppers, salami, and cheese.

3 to 4 cups

4 medium zucchini
½ cup olive oil
Salt
2 cloves garlic, finely chopped

1 tablespoon chopped fresh basil
  (or 1 teaspoon dried)
2 tablespoons minced parsley
Freshly ground black pepper
4 tablespoons red wine vinegar

Halve unpeeled zucchini and cut each half into 3 or 4 slender sticks. Heat 2 tablespoons of the oil in heavy pan or skillet and add zucchini. Stir-fry over moderate heat 2 or 3 minutes to soften slightly. Turn into a bowl or refrigerator dish and sprinkle with salt to taste (takes plenty for zucchini), garlic, basil, parsley and plenty of pepper. Mix well. Pour any oil left in frying pan into small pan and add remaining oil and vinegar. Heat to boiling and pour over zucchini. Cover and cool. Refrigerate overnight or several days.

# Antipasto Carrots

3 to 4 cups

8 medium carrots
Salt
Sugar
½ cup olive oil

1 clove garlic, minced
1 teaspoon crumbled rosemary
2 teaspoons finely chopped mint
4 tablespoons red wine vinegar

Scrape carrots and cut into 3-inch lengths. Halve and cut into slender sticks. Put in heavy saucepan with 1 inch of boiling water, ½ teaspoon salt and ¼ teaspoon sugar. Cover and simmer 5 minutes. Drain, if necessary, and turn into a bowl or refrigerator dish. Mix with olive oil. Add garlic, rosemary, mint, and vinegar. Mix gently and cover. Refrigerate overnight or several days.

47

# Fritto Misto

A lively assortment of vegetables fried crisp in a thin lacy batter. This can be fun for a table-top party in kitchen or patio using an electric fry pan.

4 to 6 servings

Egg White Batter
1 package (10 ounces) frozen
    artichoke hearts, defrosted
2 to 3 medium zucchini
Salt and pepper
2 to 3 medium carrots

1 green pepper
8 bite-size fresh mushrooms
Lemon juice
Vegetable oil for deep-frying
Lemon wedges

Make batter ahead (see recipe). Halve artichoke hearts and heat to boiling in salted water. Drain and dry on paper towels. Halve unpeeled zucchini crosswise, then cut each into 4 or 5 sticks. Sprinkle with salt and pepper. Scrape carrots, cut into 3-inch lengths, then into slender sticks. Halve green pepper, remove seeds, and cut pepper into strips. Wipe mushrooms with damp paper towels and rub with a little lemon juice. Heat oil in deep-fat fryer to 370°F. Dust vegetable pieces lightly with flour, then dip in batter. Fry a few at a time, turning as needed, until golden, crisp, and lacy looking. Remove each batch to paper towels and keep hot in 250°F. oven while you cook the rest. Heap into a napkin-lined basket and sprinkle with salt. Serve at once with lemon wedges.

## Egg White Batter

1 cup flour
1 teaspoon salt
¾ cup water
2 tablespoons olive oil
2 egg whites

Combine flour and salt and blend in water and oil with rotary beater until batter is smooth. Let stand a couple of hours. Beat egg whites until stiff. Fold into batter about 5 minutes before frying vegetables.

48

# Zucchini Potage

This creamy thick soup is patterned after the hearty peasant potages of Europe. It is filling, but light and subtly flavored. Add the cream for special occasions.

6 servings

1 leek, split, tops trimmed off
1 onion, coarsely chopped
2 tablespoons butter or margarine
1 cup diced peeled potato
3 cups water or light chicken broth
1 teaspoon salt
3 cups thinly sliced, unpeeled

zucchini (4 to 5 medium)
3 cups milk
1 teaspoon dried dill or
   1 tablespoon chopped fresh dill
Pinch of tarragon
White or black pepper
½ cup cream (optional)
Minced chives or snipped fresh dill

Wash leek under running water and chop finely. In a deep, heavy saucepan, cook onion and leek gently in melted butter until soft, but not brown, about 10 minutes. Stir frequently. Add potato, water or broth and salt. Cover and simmer 15 to 20 minutes. Add zucchini, cover, and cook until vegetables are very tender, about 15 minutes longer. Whirl in blender (in two batches, if necessary) until puréed and smooth. In same saucepan, heat milk until bubbles form around edges and stir in the purée. Add dill and tarragon. Stir over low heat until soup is very hot and flavors are well blended. Do not boil. Season with more salt if needed, a little white (or black) pepper, and stir in the cream, if you like. Heat through and ladle into warm bowls. Top with chives or dill if you have it.

## VARIATION

**Chilled Zucchini Bisque:** Make *Zucchini Potage* by preceding recipe and season with a little extra dill, some minced chives and an additional ¼ cup cream. Cool, uncovered, then pour into a bowl or refrigerator container. Cover and chill several hours. Stir bisque and adjust seasonings if necessary. (Chilling dulls the flavors somewhat). Top each bowlful with minced chives or snips of fresh dill.

# Zucchini Corn Chowder

2 cups diced, unpeeled zucchini (2 to 4 small zucchini)
2 cups water or light chicken broth
½ teaspoon salt
½ teaspoon marjoram leaves
4 slices bacon, diced
1 onion, chopped
1 tablespoon flour
1 can (1 pound) cream-style white corn
2 cups milk
Pinch of nutmeg
Freshly ground black pepper
Minced parsley or paprika

Combine zucchini, water or broth, salt and marjoram. Cover and simmer gently until tender but not mushy, about 10 minutes. Meanwhile, in deep saucepan or soup pot, cook bacon until crisp and drain on paper towels. In 2 tablespoons of the drippings (or substitute margarine if you prefer), cook onion gently until soft. Blend in flour and cook slowly about 2 minutes. Drain liquid from zucchini into mixture and stir over moderate heat until it bubbles and thickens slightly. Add zucchini, corn and milk. Season with a pinch of nutmeg, a few grindings of pepper, additional salt to taste and the bacon bits. Cook over very low heat, stirring often, until chowder is hot and flavors are mellowed together. Ladle into warm bowls and sprinkle with parsley or bright paprika.

# Curry Zucchini Soup

Zucchini seems amenable to many seasonings. Here, it makes a lovely golden soup with rice, curry and chicken broth.

4 to 5 servings

2 tablespoons butter or margarine
1 large onion, chopped
1 apple, peeled, cored, and chopped
2 teaspoons curry powder
1 quart chicken broth
¼ cup uncooked white rice

2 cups diced, unpeeled zucchini
(2 to 3 medium)
½ teaspoon salt, or to taste
1 cup milk
¼ cup heavy cream (optional)
1 tablespoon thinly sliced natural skin almonds, toasted

☛Heat butter in heavy saucepan or soup kettle. Add onion and apple and cook, stirring frequently, until they are soft. Sprinkle with curry powder, and stir and cook a few seconds. Pour in the chicken broth. Heat to boiling, drop in rice and zucchini. Season with salt (the amount depends on the saltiness of the broth). Cover pan and simmer until rice and zucchini are soft and tender, about 30 minutes. Pour into blender (in 2 batches, if necessary) and whirl until smooth. Return to pan and add milk. Heat until flavors blend. Return to pan and add milk. Heat until flavors blend. Taste and adjust seasonings as needed. Stir in cream, if used, just before serving. Ladle into warm bowls and top each with a few almond slices.

## VARIATION

**Iced Curry Zucchini Soup:** This is one of the tastiest cold soups—refreshingly delicious for warm weather dining. Make curried zucchini purée as directed in *Curry Zucchini Soup* using all ingredients except milk, cream, and almonds. Stir in milk and cream and cool the mixture. Cover and refrigerate several hours or overnight. Stir to blend soup and adjust seasonings as needed. Serve in chilled bowls with the almond topping.

# Summer Green Soup

Cool as buttermilk, pale green and refreshing. Made of puréed zucchini and buttermilk seasoned with summer herbs and chilled. Serve as an ideal low-cal lunch or supper starter.

4 servings

4 cups sliced, unpeeled young zucchini
4 sliced green onions with part of tops
1 cup light chicken broth or water
Salt
2 cups buttermilk
Freshly ground black pepper
1 tablespoon chopped fresh basil (1 teaspoon dried), or
    tarragon or green fennel tops
Minced parsley

Put zucchini and green onions in large heavy saucepan with chicken broth or boiling salted water. Cover and cook until tender, 10 to 15 minutes. Uncover for the last few minutes, if necessary, to evaporate liquid. Purée in blender and add an equal amount (2 cups) buttermilk. Blend until smooth and season to taste with salt, if needed, freshly ground pepper and finely chopped fresh (or dried) basil, tarragon or leafy green fennel tops. Cover and chill several hours to mellow flavors. Stir smooth again and adjust seasonings, if necessary. Serve in chilled bowls or cups with a topping of minced parsley or snipped green fennel tops.

# Carrot Velvet Soup

This creamy, delicate soup with subtle seasonings of cloves, white pepper and a dash of coriander is very good hot or chilled.

4 servings

2 tablespoons butter or margarine
3 whole cloves
¼ teaspoon crushed coriander seeds
3 cups sliced carrots (about 1½ pounds)
2½ cups chicken broth (or hot water and
    chicken bouillon cubes)
¼ teaspoon salt
¼ teaspoon sugar
White pepper to taste
1 cup half-and-half
Chives or minced parsley

Put butter, cloves and coriander seeds into a deep saucepan. Add carrots, chicken broth, a pinch each of salt and sugar and a generous dash of white pepper. Cover and cook gently until carrots are very tender, about 30 minutes. Pour mixture into blender container (in two batches if necessary) and whirl until smooth. In the same saucepan, heat half-and-half briefly and stir in the carrot purée. Heat just to boiling, add a little more salt and white pepper, if needed. Serve hot with a topping of chopped chives or parsley.

### VARIATION

**Chilled Carrot Bisque:** Make carrot purée according to directions for *Carrot Velvet Soup*. Combine with half-and-half. Chill in a covered bowl several hours or overnight. Stir again and add additional salt, white pepper, and cream, if necessary. (Chilling thickens soup and often dulls flavors.) Serve in chilled bowls topped with minced chives or parsley.

# Pioneer Carrot Soup

This is an old-fashioned carrot soup with the homey snap of crisp, salt pork bits.

6 servings

*2 pounds carrots, sliced (about 4 cups)*
*½ cup chopped celery*
*1 onion, chopped*
*Salt*
*Pinch of sugar*
*3 cups water or light chicken broth*
*6 whole black peppercorns*
*1 broken bay leaf*
*¼ pound salt pork, chopped*
*¼ cup flour*
*3 cups milk*
*Dash of cayenne pepper*

Put carrots, celery, onion, 1 teaspoon salt, sugar, water or broth, peppercorns and bay leaf in a large deep saucepan. Cover and cook until carrots are very tender, about 30 minutes. Whirl in blender with cooking liquid (in two batches if necessary) until puréed. In same saucepan, cook salt pork until browned and crisp. Stir in flour until smooth and cook over low heat about 2 minutes. Add milk and a dash of cayenne pepper. Cook over low heat, stirring, until sauce boils and thickens. Season to taste with salt. Add carrot purée and heat slowly until flavors are blended.

# Solid Gold Soup

The gold here is edible and delicious in a vitalizing cold soup of carrots and orange juice that is blender easy.

4 servings

½ cup minced onion
1 strip orange peel (yellow only), ½ by 2 inches
2 tablespoons butter or margarine
1 tablespoon flour
2 cups sliced, scraped carrots
2½ cups water
2 teaspoons sugar
½ teaspoon salt
¼ teaspoon ground ginger
¼ teaspoon ground cloves
1½ cups orange juice
1 tablespoon lemon juice
White pepper to taste
¼ cup sour cream, sweet cream, or yogurt
Finely chopped mint or chives

Cook onion and orange strip slowly in butter until soft but not brown. Smooth in flour, then stir in carrots, water, sugar, salt and spices. Cover and cook gently until tender enough to purée, 10 to 15 minutes. Whirl in blender until smoothly puréed. Blend in remaining ingredients except mint or chives. Taste and add more salt and lemon juice, if needed. Cover and chill several hours. Serve cold in small bowls or cups with chopped mint or chives on top.

# Soupe au Pistou

A paste of basil, garlic, cheese and olive oil gives this great French vegetable soup its distinctive flavor. In winter, it may contain several kinds of beans; in summer, use fresh vegetables such as carrots, peas, and zucchini. It makes a delightful meal with French bread and cheese.

8 servings

1 onion, diced
1 leek, trimmed, split,
    carefully washed, and chopped
5 tablespoons olive oil, divided
3 quarts boiling water
1 tablespoon salt
2 cups diced scraped carrots
1 cup diced peeled potatoes

2 cups cut green beans
3 tomatoes, peeled and diced
3 medium zucchini, diced
Freshly ground black pepper
4 cloves garlic, chopped
¼ cup chopped fresh basil
    (or 1 tablespoon dried basil)
½ cup freshly grated
    Parmesan cheese

In a deep heavy soup pot or kettle, cook onion and leek gently in 2 tablespoons of olive oil until soft and golden. Add boiling water, salt, carrots, potatoes, green beans and tomatoes (add frozen beans later). Cover and simmer about 30 minutes. Add zucchini and additional hot water if needed (and frozen beans, if used). Cover and cook 30 minutes longer, or until vegetables are tender but still retain their shape. Add more salt, if needed, and freshly ground pepper.

To make *pistou*, crush garlic with wooden spoon or with mortar and pestle and gradually pound in basil to a fairly smooth paste. Work in ¼ cup Parmesan and, bit by bit, blend in the remaining 3 tablespoons of olive oil. Blend a few spoonfuls of hot soup into the paste, then stir the paste back into soup. Heat through to blend flavors. Adjust seasonings if necessary. Ladle into warm soup bowls and sprinkle with the rest of the cheese.

# 3

# Omelets, Quiches, and Casseroles

# Zucchini Green Chile Quiche

A French quiche goes international with American cheeses, Mexican chiles, and Italian squash. The flavor has great delicacy but is spirited at the same time—completely different.

6 main-dish servings
12 appetizer wedges

*Pastry for 9-inch pie crust (your own or a mix)*
*3 cups coarsely grated, unpeeled zucchini (about ¾ pound)*
*Salt*
*1 can (4 ounces) whole green chiles*
  *(do not use pre-diced chiles)*
*¾ cup sliced green onions and tops (about 6)*
*1½ tablespoons butter or margarine*
*1 tablespoon flour*
*1 cup grated cheddar cheese*
*½ cup shredded Monterey Jack cheese*
*3 eggs*
*1½ cups undiluted evaporated milk (or cream)*
*Freshly ground black pepper*

Roll pastry a little thicker than for pies and fit into 9-inch glass pie pan or 10-inch fluted quiche dish. Trim pastry even with top for quiche dish. For pie pan, trim pastry with ½ inch overhang. Turn it under and press to rim with fork. Grate the zucchini on a sheet of foil and sprinkle with salt. Let stand 30 minutes, then squeeze out moisture and blot dry. Rinse and seed chiles, blot dry, and cut into ½ inch pieces. Cook green onions slowly in melted butter, about 1 minute. Stir in zucchini and heat a few moments only, until zucchini is glazed with fat. Blend in flour, then spread in pastry shell. Sprinkle with half the cheeses and the chiles. Beat eggs with milk and season lightly with salt and pepper. Pour into pastry shell and sprinkle with remaining cheeses. Bake at 400°F. for 15 minutes. Reduce heat to 350°F. and bake about 20 to 25 minutes longer, until custard is set and slightly puffed. Cool at least 15 minutes before cutting.

# Zucchini Bacon Quiche

This is a main-dish cheese pie made like the classic Quiche Lorraine with the fresh, garden flavor of zucchini added.

6 main-dish servings
12 appetizer wedges

*Pastry for 9-inch pie crust (your own or a mix)*
*2½ cups coarsely grated unpeeled zucchini (4 to 6 zucchini)*
*Salt*
*4 slices bacon, diced*
*½ cup chopped onion*
*1½ tablespoons margarine or bacon drippings*
*1 tablespoon flour*
*1½ cups shredded Swiss cheese*
*3 eggs*
*1½ cups milk or undiluted evaporated milk*
*Freshly ground black pepper*

Roll pastry a little thicker than for pies and fit into a 9-inch glass pie dish or a 10-inch fluted quiche dish. Trim evenly in quiche dish. For pie dish, trim pastry with ½ inch overhang. Turn it under and press to rim with fork. Grate zucchini onto sheet of foil and sprinkle with salt. Let stand 30 minutes. Squeeze out excess moisture and blot dry with paper towels. Cook bacon until crisp. Drain on paper towels. In same pan, in 1½ tablespoons margarine or bacon drippings, cook onion gently until soft and golden. Stir in flour and zucchini, heat a minute or two to glaze with fat. Spread half the cheese and bacon in pastry shell. Beat eggs with milk and stir in zucchini. Season lightly with salt and pepper. Pour into pastry shell and sprinkle with rest of bacon and cheese. Bake at 400°F. for 15 minutes. Reduce heat to 350°F. and bake 20 to 25 minutes longer, until custard is set and slightly puffed. Cool 15 to 20 minutes before cutting.

## NOTE

May be baked ahead and reheated at 350°F. for 20 to 30 minutes.

# Tomato Zucchini Pie

This is much like a quiche, but not so rich. Refrigerated crescent rolls are used to make the easy pie shell.

6 main-dish servings

2 cups sliced zucchini (2 to 3 small)
1 small onion, thinly sliced
2 tablespoons olive or vegetable oil
1 to 2 tomatoes
1 can (8 ounces) refrigerated crescent rolls
2 tablespoons dry bread crumbs
Salt and pepper
½ teaspoon oregano
1½ tablespoons butter or margarine
Flour
2 eggs, beaten
1 cup milk
¼ cup shredded Swiss cheese
¼ cup grated Parmesan cheese

Cut unpeeled zucchini into 1/8-inch slices. Separate onion slices into rings. Heat oil in heavy skillet. Add onion and zucchini and stir-fry over low heat until onion is soft and zucchini tinged with brown, about 5 minutes. Slice tomatoes about ⅓-inch thick and lay on paper towels to blot dry. Unroll crescent rolls, lay on board, and arrange in shape to fit into 9-inch glass pie pan. Lay in pan and press edges together to form a crust in bottom and on sides of dish. Sprinkle with bread crumbs and cover with zucchini and onions. Season with salt, pepper and oregano. Heat butter in the same frying pan. Dip tomato slices lightly in flour and fry in the butter until tinged with brown on each side, just a minute or two. Lay evenly over zucchini. Beat eggs with milk and season—very lightly—with salt and pepper, then pour over vegetables. Sprinkle top with mixed Swiss and Parmesan cheeses. Bake at 350°F. 40 to 45 minutes, or until filling is set and crust richly browned.

# Zucchini Soufflé

Grated zucchini rather than the usual cooked purée gives this light and delicately flavored soufflé a different quality.

4 to 5 servings

*2 to 3 small zucchini (1 cup grated)*
*Salt*
*3 tablespoons butter or margarine, divided*
*2 tablespoons minced green onions or shallots*
*3 tablespoons flour*
*¾ cup milk*
*½ teaspoon salt*
*White pepper or a few grains cayenne*
*½ teaspoon dried dill or basil*
*4 whole eggs*
*½ cup shredded Swiss cheese*
*1 extra egg white*

Coarsely grate unpeeled zucchini onto sheet of foil (measure 1 cup) and sprinkle lightly with salt. Let stand about 20 minutes. Press and squeeze out excess moisture. Melt 1 tablespoon of the butter in a small heavy saucepan. Add green onions or shallots and cook gently until soft. Add zucchini and stir over low heat until well coated with fat and most of moisture has cooked out, 2 or 3 minutes. Transfer onions and zucchini to small bowl. In the same pan, melt 2 tablespoons of butter and blend in flour. Cook a minute or two without browning, then add milk. Stir over moderate heat until sauce boils and thickens. Season with salt, white pepper or cayenne, and dill or basil. Beat in egg yolks, one at a time, stir in zucchini and cheese, leaving 1 tablespoon cheese for the top. Beat egg whites with a pinch of salt until they stand in upright peaks when beater is withdrawn. Stir a big spoonful of egg whites into sauce and blend it in lightly. Fold in the rest of the egg whites quickly and lightly. Turn into a greased 6-cup, straight-sided soufflé dish or casserole. Sprinkle with remaining cheese. Bake at 375°F. for 30 to 35 minutes, until puffed and lightly browned. Serve at once.

# Zucchini Puff Casserole

This fluffy casserole with a garden fresh taste is somewhat like a soufflé, but much easier to make and less tempermental.

4 to 6 servings

8 unpeeled medium zucchini (about 2 pounds)
Water
Salt
1 clove garlic, chopped
¼ cup melted butter or margarine
½ cup finely minced onion
4 eggs, lightly beaten
½ cup coarse dry bread crumbs
1 cup grated cheddar cheese
Freshly ground black pepper
2 tablespoons grated dry bread crumbs for top
2 teaspoons melted butter for top

Scrub zucchini, remove tips, halve lengthwise, and slice. Place in saucepan with ½ inch of boiling water, ¾ teaspoon salt, and garlic. Cover and cook gently until tender, about 10 minutes. Drain and put zucchini in large mixing bowl (use electric mixer, if you have one). Beat until coarsely puréed with pieces of bright green zucchini skin still evident. Mix in butter, onion and eggs. Fold in coarse bread crumbs and cheese. Add pepper to taste and additional salt if needed. Scoop into a well-buttered 1½-quart baking dish. Top with grated crumbs and drizzle melted butter over them. Bake at 350°F. about 45 minutes, until slightly puffed and browned.

# Zucchini Corn Casserole

Made like corn pudding, this dish has the extra asset of pretty, green zucchini slices. It is especially good with chicken or pork.

6 servings

4 cups sliced, unpeeled zucchini (4 to 5 medium)
2 tablespoons butter or margarine
1 onion, chopped
1 clove garlic, minced
Salt and pepper
2 tablespoons hot water
1 tablespoon chopped parsley
1 can (1 pound) cream-style corn
1 cup grated cheddar cheese, divided
4 eggs, beaten

Slice zucchini and blot dry on paper towels. Heat butter in heavy skillet and add onion. Cook gently, stirring often until soft. Add zucchini and garlic, stir until slices are well coated. Season with about ½ teaspoon salt, pepper to taste, and add hot water. Cover and steam until tender, about 10 minutes. Stir frequently to prevent sticking. Remove from heat and add parsley, corn, ½ cup cheese (save rest for top) and beaten eggs. Mix well and pour into well-buttered 1½-quart casserole. Top with remaining cheese. Bake at 350°F. 45 to 50 minutes, until mixture is set and slightly puffed.

SEE ALSO *Zucchini Cheese Loaf* (p. 172)

# Tortino di Zucchini

This baked Italian omelet makes a tempting light dish for luncheon, brunch or supper. The texture resembles a soufflé rather than a French omelet. Fruit and a salad with French bread are good served with it.

4 servings

2 small zucchini (about 1 cup sliced)
Flour
4 green onions
1 tablespoon olive or other light oil
2 tablespoons butter or margarine
½ cup slivered Canadian bacon or ham
  (omit for vegetable omelet)
6 eggs
⅓ cup undiluted evaporated milk
Salt and freshly ground black pepper
½ teaspoon dried marjoram leaves, crumbled
½ teaspoon dried sweet basil leaves, crumbled
⅓ cup grated Parmesan cheese

Wash and trim zucchini, halve lengthwise, and cut into diagonal slices. Dust lightly with flour. Slice green onions and 2 or 3 inches of the tops. Butter generously a shallow round (1½-quart) dish and place in 350°F. oven while you mix the omelet. Heat half the oil and butter in a small heavy skillet. Toss in onion and bacon slivers or ham strips. Stir over gentle heat a couple of minutes. Push to side of pan and add the remaining oil and butter. When hot, add zucchini and stir over moderate heat until lightly browned. Beat eggs with milk just enough to mix well. Season them with salt, pepper and herbs. Spread zucchini mix in hot baking dish and pour eggs over it. Mix lightly and sprinkle with cheese. Bake at 350°F. until set and slightly puffed, 15 to 20 minutes. Do not overbake. Cut in wedges and serve hot from baking dish.

SEE ALSO *Zucchini Frittata* (p. 170)

# Zucchini Green Chile Scramble

If you're not a green-chile fan (as I am), use diced green bell peppers instead. Each makes a delicious contribution to the dish. Serve with crisply toasted English muffins for breakfast or brunch.

3 to 4 servings

6 slices lean bacon, diced
6 green onions, sliced
2 small zucchini (about 1 cup), sliced
6 eggs
6 tablespoons light cream or evaporated milk
Salt and freshly ground black pepper
½ teaspoon Worcestershire sauce
1 to 2 whole, canned green chiles, seeded and diced
¾ cup diced Monterey Jack or cheddar cheese

Fry bacon in large heavy skillet until crisp. Drain on paper towels. Pour off all but 2 tablespoons of the drippings. Add green onions and zucchini to pan. Stir-fry until onions are soft and zucchini crisp-tender, 2 or 3 minutes. Add bacon. Beat eggs lightly with milk and season with salt, pepper, and Worcestershire sauce. Add chiles and pour into skillet. Top with cheese. Cook over low heat just a few minutes, stirring very gently and lifting eggs from the bottom till cheese melts and eggs are soft and fluffy. Serve at once, on warm plates, with toasted English muffins.

# Hamburger Zucchini Scramble

You can cook this meal-in-a-skillet in minutes. It is especially good served with split and toasted French rolls.

4 servings

1½ cups coarsely diced, unpeeled zucchini (2 to 3 medium)
Flour
2 tablespoons olive oil
½ cup finely chopped onion
1 clove garlic, minced
¾ pound ground lean beef
Salt and pepper
8 eggs
⅓ cup light cream or evaporated milk
Grated Parmesan cheese

Toss zucchini with about 2 teaspoons flour to coat lightly. Heat oil in large heavy skillet and stir-fry zucchini with onion and garlic until onion is soft and zucchini lightly browned. Crumble in beef, a little at a time, and stir-fry until lightly browned. Season mixture with salt and pepper to taste. Beat eggs lightly with cream and season with salt and pepper. Pour into pan. Cook and stir gently over low heat until eggs are set, but still soft and creamy. Sprinkle with Parmesan and serve at once.

# Zucchini Paysanne

Combine the flavors and colors of a country garden and bake in a casserole. Serve it as a side dish with grilled chicken, lamb or hamburger—or alone with French bread and fruit for a pleasant luncheon.

4 to 6 servings

4 medium zucchini
Salt
2 tablespoons cracker crumbs
Freshly ground black pepper
2 to 3 medium tomatoes, sliced
1 onion, chopped
Chopped fresh sweet basil or dried basil, to taste
1 tablespoon minced parsley
1 cup grated cheddar or Swiss cheese
2 tablespoons olive oil
¼ cup grated Parmesan cheese

Remove tips from zucchini, place in deep saucepan with ½ inch boiling salted water. Cover and cook gently 5 minutes only. Drain, rinse quickly in cool water, then cut into lengthwise slices. Sprinkle a large greased baking dish with cracker crumbs. Use half the zucchini to make the bottom layer. Season well with salt, pepper and a little dill. Add a layer of tomatoes, about half the onion, and season with salt, pepper, a little basil, and minced parsley. Sprinkle with half the cheese. Finish by adding the rest of the zucchini, onion, seasonings, and tomatoes. Pour olive oil over all to give vegetables a shiny look. Combine Parmesan with the remaining cheese and sprinkle on top. Bake at 375°F. about 45 minutes, or until vegetables are crisp-tender and top is lightly browned.

SEE ALSO French Casserole (p. 167)
Zucchini Green Chile Casserole (p. 171)

# Creamed Zucchini Gratiné

An easy new way to make a creamed vegetable, this one is fresh-tasting and nutritious. Simply stir shredded, raw zucchini into a cream sauce, top with crumbs, and bake a few minutes.

4 servings

3 cups shredded raw, unpeeled zucchini (4 to 6 medium)
Salt
1 onion, finely chopped
3 tablespoons butter or margarine
1 clove garlic, finely minced
3 tablespoons flour
1½ cups milk
½ teaspoon seasoned salt
Freshly ground black pepper
½ teaspoon crushed dried marjoram
¼ cup sour cream
¼ cup buttered dry bread crumbs

Grate zucchini onto a sheet of foil and sprinkle with salt. Let stand 30 minutes. Cook onion in melted butter until soft and golden, at least 5 minutes. Add garlic and blend in flour. Stir over low heat about 2 minutes more, but do not brown. Add milk and cook over medium heat, stirring constantly until sauce bubbles and thickens. Season with seasoned salt, additional plain salt to taste (about ½ teaspoon), and a few grindings of pepper and marjoram. Squeeze excess moisture from zucchini and stir into sauce along with sour cream. Turn into baking dish and top with buttered crumbs. Heat in 350°F. oven until browned on top, about 30 minutes.

# Stuffed Zucchini

These are delicious and can be infinitely varied. Large vegetables, (8-inch size) are more practical, especially if served as an entree for luncheon or supper. You will find this a tasty way to use up bits of leftover cooked meat or fish.

# Ham Stuffed Zucchini

This is my favorite stuffing, with eggs beaten separately to make a fluffy light filling.

4 servings

4 large zucchini
Salt
Vegetable oil
½ onion, finely chopped
2 tablespoons butter or margarine
1 cup soft bread crumbs
1 cup finely chopped cooked ham
Pinch of allspice
1 teaspoon marjoram
Freshly ground black pepper
2 eggs, separated
¾ cup grated cheddar cheese

Put zucchini in wide heavy pan or skillet with 1 inch of boiling water and 1 teaspoon salt. Cover and steam until nearly tender, 7 to 10 minutes. Drain and rinse quickly in cold water to stop cooking. Cut in halves lengthwise and scoop out centers with a teaspoon, leaving a ¼-inch shell. Chop centers. Turn shells upside down on paper towels to dry. Rub lightly with oil. Cook onion in melted butter until soft. Add chopped zucchini, bread crumbs, ham and seasonings. Stir over low heat a minute or two.

Blend in beaten egg yolks and half the cheese. Beat whites until stiff and fold in. Place shells in shallow pan. Spoon in stuffing and sprinkle with rest of cheese. Bake at 350°F. about 30 minutes.

### VARIATION

**Sausage Stuffed Zucchini:** Make same as preceding *Ham Stuffed Zucchini.* Substitute 1 cup cooked pork sausage (fresh Italian sausage is delicious here also) for the ham. Beat in whole eggs lightly.

# Stuffed Zucchini, Middle East

4 servings

*Cooked zucchini shells (from 4 large zucchini)*
*½ cup chopped onion*
*Olive oil or vegetable oil*
*½ pound ground, lean lamb*
*Salt and pepper*
*Dash of cinnamon*
*2 tablespoons chopped parsley*
*1 small tomato, chopped*
*¾ cup cooked rice*
*2 tablespoons pine nuts or chopped walnuts (optional)*
*1 can (8 ounces) tomato sauce*
*½ cup water or stock*

Prepare zucchini shells as described in *Ham Stuffed Zucchini.* For the filling, cook onion with chopped zucchini pulp from centers in a little oil until soft. Add lamb, and brown lightly. Season with salt, pepper, a dash of cinnamon, and parsley. Mix with tomato, rice and pine nuts. Heap into zucchini shells and set in shallow pan. Drizzle with a little oil. Pour in tomato sauce diluted with ½ cup water or stock. Bake at 350°F. 30 to 45 minutes, basting occasionally with sauce.

# Cheese Stuffed Zucchini

4 main-dish servings
8 side-dish portions

4 large zucchini
Vegetable oil
4 slices bacon, diced
1 small onion, chopped
1 clover garlic, chopped
1 cup soft bread crumbs
½ teaspoon basil
1 tablespoon minced parsley
Freshly ground black pepper
1 cup grated cheddar cheese
2 eggs, beaten

Steam and scoop out the zucchini following directions given in *Ham Stuffed Zucchini*. Drain as directed and rub with oil. Fry bacon until crisp and drain on paper towels. In same pan, in 2 tablespoons of the drippings, cook onion and garlic until soft but not brown. Stir in chopped zucchini centers and cook a minute or two. Mix in bread crumbs, basil, parsley, plenty of black pepper and half the cheese and bacon. Stir in beaten eggs. Place zucchini shells in shallow pan and heap with stuffing. Sprinkle cheese and bacon over the tops. Bake at 350°F. about 30 minutes.

# Zucchini Swiss Crêpes

*There are 3 parts to the recipe, but all can be made ahead and heated just before serving.*

Lacy thin pancakes stuffed with gentle flavored zucchini and ricotta cheese, topped with cheese sauce and glazed. This makes a pretty and nourishing dish for a luncheon or a first course for a company dinner.

4 to 6 servings
(2 to 3 crêpes each)

1 recipe Crêpes
2½ cups coarsely shredded, unpeeled zucchini
6 tablespoons chopped green onions and tops
4 tablespoons butter or margarine, divided
Salt
1 cup ricotta cheese or well-drained, fine-curd cottage cheese
Pinch each of sweet basil and oregano (or 1 teaspoon dried dill)
Freshly ground black pepper
¾ cup shredded Swiss cheese, divided
2 tablespoons flour
1½ cups milk
Nutmeg

Make crêpes ahead as directed in recipe. Shred zucchini and lightly press out excess moisture. Cook onions gently in 2 tablespoons of the butter until soft. Add zucchini and stir-fry until coated with butter. Season with ½ teaspoon salt, cover and cook slowly until crisp-tender, about 5 minutes. Stir or shake pan frequently. Uncover and cook a few seconds to evaporate any excess liquids. Mix with ricotta or drained cottage cheese. Season ricotta mixture with a generous pinch each of oregano and basil, the cottage cheese with dill. Mix well and add a few grindings of pepper and ¼ cup of the Swiss cheese. Put about 2 tablespoons of the filling on bottom third of each crêpe and roll it up. Place seam-side down and one-layer deep in shallow baking dish. Cover and refrigerate until later or finish with sauce as follows. Melt 2 tablespoons butter and blend in flour.

Stir over low heat without browning, about 2 minutes. Add milk and stir with whisk over low heat until sauce boils and is smooth and thickened. Season with ½ teaspoon salt, a pinch of nutmeg and ¼ cup of the Swiss cheese. Spread over filled crêpes and sprinkle with remaining cheese. Place under broiler about 5 minutes, or until sauce is bubbly hot and beautifully flecked with brown. Serve from dish.

## For the Crêpes

18 (5½ to 6 inch) crêpes

1½ cups milk
3 eggs
¾ cup all-purpose flour
¼ teaspoon salt
1½ tablespoons melted butter or margarine
Butter for frying

To make in blender, put in milk, then eggs, flour, salt and butter. Cover and whirl at high speed 1 minute, or until batter is smooth. Or in bowl, beat eggs with whisk or beaters, slowly add flour and beat until smooth. Gradually beat in milk, salt and butter. Stir until batter is smooth—strain if you can't get out the lumps. Cover and refrigerate at least 2 hours or longer. Heat small iron skillet or crêpe pan (5½ - 6 inches) until a drop of butter sizzles on contact. Brush with butter. With one hand, pour in 2½ to 3 tablespoons batter, and with other hand quickly tilt and turn pan so batter coats bottom evenly and covers holes formed by bubbles. (I dip out batter with my handled ¼ cup measure, judging after the first crêpe exactly how much batter I need.) Cook until top looks dryish and underside is golden, about ½ minute. You can lift edge with finger and see. Turn and cook second side a few seconds, until lightly splotched with brown. Stack between sheets of wax paper. Cover and keep at room temperature until ready to assemble the dish, or wrap in foil and refrigerate or freeze for a few weeks only, 6 to a stack.

### NOTE

If you make and fill crêpes ahead (and you should), make sauce also. Cool it with a piece of foil pressed directly on its surface, then refrigerate. Heat slightly just before serving and spread on crêpes.

74

# Carrot Soufflé

Finely chopped carrots give this airy soufflé a flavor and a texture slightly different from the traditional puréed vegetable soufflé. Excellent non-meat main dish for luncheon or supper.

4 to 5 servings

*1 cup finely chopped cooked carrots (4 to 5 medium)*
*Salt*
*Sugar*
*3 tablespoons chopped green onions*
*3 tablespoons butter or margarine*
*3 tablespoons flour*
*¾ cup milk*
*White pepper to taste*
*Dash of nutmeg*
*½ teaspoon thyme*
*1 tablespoon minced parsley*
*4 eggs, separated*
*½ cup shredded Swiss cheese*
*1 extra egg white*

Cook scraped carrots in a covered pan in a small amount of boiling salted water with a pinch of sugar, until tender, 15 to 20 minutes. Drain, if necessary, and chop finely. In small heavy saucepan, cook onions in melted butter until soft but not brown. Blend in flour and stir over low heat about 2 minutes. Remove from heat, add milk all at once. Stir and return to heat. Cook and stir until sauce boils and thickens. Season with ¾ teaspoon salt, white pepper, nutmeg, thyme and parsley. Beat in egg yolks one at a time, then fold in cheese and carrots. Wash beaters and beat egg whites until stiff but still moist. Add a little of the sauce to egg whites and blend in. Fold whites lightly and quickly into rest of carrot mixture. Pour into well-buttered, straight-sided 6-cup soufflé dish or casserole. Bake at 375°F. 30 to 35 minutes, until soufflé is puffed above top of dish and has browned lightly. Serve at once.

# Carrot Bacon Casserole

Mashed cooked carrots sparked with onion and bacon are puffed to soufflé lightness with beaten eggs. Delightful with meat, this casserole can also be served as a luncheon entrée with salad and rolls.

6 servings

*4 cups sliced, scraped carrots*
*Salt*
*Sugar*
*4 slices bacon, cut in pieces*
*½ cup finely chopped onion*
*2 tablespoons butter or margarine*
*⅓ cup half-and-half or milk*
*White or black pepper*
*Dash of ground ginger*
*3 eggs, lightly beaten*

Put carrots in heavy saucepan with 1-inch of boiling water and ½ teaspoon each of salt and sugar. Cover and cook until tender enough to mash, 15 to 20 minutes. Drain, if necessary, or uncover last few minutes to evaporate liquids. Cook bacon until crisp. Drain on paper towels. In 1 tablespoon of the drippings, cook onion until soft but do not allow it to brown. Mash carrots until smooth, in mixer or with a wire whisk with butter and milk. Whip until smooth and light. Season with salt, pepper, and ginger to taste. Stir in onions and half the bacon bits. Beat in eggs. Turn into a greased baking dish and top with rest of bacon bits. Bake at 375°F., until puffed and firm, 30 to 40 minutes.

# Carrot Kugel

A delicate, soufflé-like pudding from Jewish cookery. It makes an unusual accompaniment for meats or it can be served as a nice light meatless luncheon entrée. If served for Passover, use potato flour or a mixture of potato flour and matzo meal, instead of the wheat flour. Like all soufflés, this will lose some of its billowy fluff if allowed to sit around after being taken from the oven, so serve immediately!

6 servings

1 cup grated raw carrots, tightly packed
½ cup sugar
¼ cup coarsely shredded apple
6 tablespoons all-purpose flour
   (or 4½ tablespoons potato flour)
1 teaspoon grated fresh lemon peel
2 tablespoons fresh lemon juice
2 tablespoons white dinner wine
4 eggs, separated
Pinch of salt

Combine carrots, sugar, apple, flour, lemon peel, juice and wine. Mix well and blend in lightly beaten egg yolks. Beat egg whites with a pinch of salt until they stand in stiff peaks when beaters are withdrawn. Gently and quickly fold into carrot mixture. Spoon lightly into oiled 1½-quart soufflé dish or casserole. Bake in preheated (375°F.) oven until puffed and golden, 30 to 35 minutes. Serve at once.

# Rice Carrot Bake

Plenty hearty for a non-meat main dish, this may be served as a vegetable with light meats such as fish or chicken.

4 to 6 servings

1 cup cooked rice (⅓ cup uncooked)
¼ cup finely chopped onion
¼ cup finely chopped celery
2 tablespoons vegetable oil
2 cups shredded raw carrots
2 tablespoons chopped parsley
½ teaspoon dried marjoram
Salt and pepper
½ cup grated cheddar or Swiss cheese
3 eggs, beaten
¼ cup grated Parmesan cheese

Cook rice ahead of time (by package directions) or use leftover rice. Cook onion and celery in hot oil until soft. Add carrots, parsley, rice and marjoram. Stir over low heat until heated through. Season to taste with salt and pepper. Fold in cheddar or Swiss cheese and beaten eggs. Turn into greased shallow baking dish and top with Parmesan. Bake at 350°F. until firmish and lightly browned on top, 35 to 45 minutes. Cut into wedges and serve from baking dish.

# Carrot Tzimmes

Carrots in some form are a tradition for many Jewish holiday meals. They may be cooked with meats or prepared with fruits or other vegetables as a side dish. Often they are lightly spiced and sweetened with honey as in this recipe.

6 servings

2 or 3 medium sweet potatoes (1 pound)
6 medium carrots (1 pound)
Salt
3 tablespoons margarine
¼ teaspoon ground ginger
¼ teaspoon ground nutmeg
Freshly ground black pepper to taste
2 tart cooking apples (Pippins are good)
3 tablespoons honey

Peel and slice potatoes. Scrape and slice carrots. Put both in saucepan with 1 cup of boiling water, ½ teaspoon salt. Cover and cook gently until tender, about 25 minutes. Drain, if necessary, or uncover and cook a few moments to evaporate excess liquid. Whip with electric beaters until smooth and season with 1 tablespoon of the margarine, the ginger, nutmeg and pepper. Add salt if needed. Whip until very smooth and light. Spread about ⅓ of the mixture in a greased baking dish. Quarter the apples, core, and peel. Slice thinly and spread half the slices on carrots. Dot with part of the margarine and drizzle with half the honey. Spread with another third of the carrot mixture, the rest of the apples slices, dots of margarine and the honey. Spread with carrot mixture and dot with margarine. Bake at 350°F. 40 to 45 minutes. Serve warm.

# Mixed Vegetables Mornay

This is my answer for a make-ahead vegetable casserole I can carry to our family Christmas party. It reheats while we make gravy, and set out the relishes, salads and such.

6 to 8 servings

*6 to 8 young carrots (1 pound)*
*2 cups celery in 2-inch pieces*
*2 cups chicken broth (homemade or from bouillon cubes)*
*1 dozen small whole onions*
*Salt*
*3 tablespoons butter or margarine*
*3 tablespoons flour*
*1½ cups milk*
*Freshly ground black pepper*
*Nutmeg*
*Pinch of marjoram or thyme*
*¼ cup coarse dry bread crumbs*
*4 tablespoons grated Parmesan cheese*

Scrape carrots and cut into 2-inch pieces. Halve or quarter lengthwise the larger carrots. Put in heavy saucepan with celery and chicken broth. Cover and simmer until tender, 15 to 20 minutes. Drain off broth and save it. Transfer carrots and celery to buttered 2-quart casserole. At same time, cook onions in boiling salted water until nearly tender, 15 to 20 minutes. Drain onions and add to casserole. Melt butter in small saucepan and blend in flour. Cook over low heat, without browning, about 2 minutes. Add broth and milk. Cook, stirring over low heat, until sauce is smooth and thickened. Season with salt and pepper to taste and a pinch each of nutmeg and marjoram. Stir in 2 tablespoons Parmesan and pour sauce over vegetables. Mix rest of Parmesan and bread crumbs, spread over top. Bake at 350°F. about 30 minutes.

# 4

# *Light-Touch Main Dishes*

# Chicken and Zucchini, Vermouth

Parmesan cheese, Vermouth and cream combine beautifully to make a subtle, velvety sauce for browned chicken and delicate green zucchini chunks. Serve with rice or French bread.

4 servings

1 frying chicken (about 2½ pounds) disjoinied or
   2 to 3 pounds meaty pieces of fryer chicken
Fresh lemon juice
Salt and freshly ground black pepper
¼ cup flour
6 tablespoons grated Parmesan cheese
2 tablespoons butter or margarine
2 teaspoons light salad oil
1 clove garlic
3 or 4 green onions or shallots, chopped
4 to 5 small young zucchini (4 to 5 inches long)
¼ cup dry Vermouth (or dry white table wine
   such as Chenin Blanc)
1 cup light cream
2 tablespoons minced parsley


Sprinkle chicken with lemon juice and season with salt and pepper. Combine flour and ¼ cup Parmesan. Roll chicken in mixture to coat evenly. Heat butter and oil in heavy frying pan, add chicken, and brown on both sides, turning as necessary. Remove to 2-quart casserole and grate garlic over it. In 1 tablespoon of fat drippings in frying pan, cook onions or shallots a few minutes, until soft. Remove tips from zucchini and cut into chunks ½ to ¾ inch thick. Stir in pan until coated with fat. Add Vermouth, stir up brown particles from bottom and blend in cream and parsley. When hot, pour over chicken. Tuck zucchini chunks around chicken under sauce. Sprinkle remaining Parmesan over all and cover dish. Bake in 350°F. oven until chicken and zucchini are tender, 30 to 40 minutes (uncover last 10 minutes). Zucchini should retain color and shape.

# Country Garden Fish

Sandwich a lemony rice stuffing between your favorite fish fillets and bake with bright topping of tomatoes, onion and zucchini.

6 servings

1 small onion, chopped
4 tablespoons butter or margarine, divided
1 cup cooked rice
2 tablespoons chopped parsley
Lemon juice
Salt and freshly ground black pepper
1½ to 2 pounds fish fillets
1½ cups coarsely diced, unpeeled zucchini
2 cups coarsely chopped fresh tomatoes
2 teaspoons chopped fresh sweet basil (or ½ teaspoon dried)
2 teaspoons chopped fresh dill (or ½ teaspoon dried)

Cook half the onion in 2 tablespoons butter until soft. Add rice, parsley, about 1 tablespoon lemon juice, salt and pepper to taste. Stir over low heat until well mixed. Rub fish with lemon juice and season with salt and pepper. Put half the fillets in shallow greased baking dish and cover with rice mixture. Top with rest of fish. Cook remaining onion and zucchini in rest of butter in same pan until shiny and softened, 2 or 3 minutes. Add tomatoes, herbs and salt and pepper to taste. Stir over low heat 2 or 3 minutes and pour over fish. Drizzle with a little additional butter if you like. Bake at 375°F. 25 to 30 minutes. Serve from dish.

# Broiled Liver and Zucchini Strips

4 medium zucchini                                                    4 servings
1 pound beef or calf's liver in ½-inch thick slices
Salt and pepper
Melted butter, margarine, oil, or bacon drippings
2 eggs, beaten
Milk
2 to 3 cups fine dry bread crumbs
Lemon wedges

Slice zucchini lengthwise into flat slices ¼ inch thick. Blot dry on paper towels. Cut liver slices into strips about 2 inches wide  Dry on paper towels, season with salt and pepper and dip in melted butter, margarine, fresh bacon drippings or vegetable oil. Place on buttered or oiled cookie sheet. Season zucchini slices with salt and dip in egg beaten with 2 tablespoons milk or water, then roll to coat evenly with fine dry bread crumbs. Lay on the cookie sheet and drizzle lightly with one of the fats. Broil 4 to 6 inches from heat until zucchini is golden and tender, the liver browned and moist inside, about 5 to 6 minutes. No need to turn them. Serve at once with wedges of fresh lemon.

## VARIATIONS

**Sautéed Liver and Zucchini Strips:** Cut liver and zucchini in strips as described in preceding recipe. Season liver with salt and pepper and dip lightly in flour, shake off excess. Dip zucchini in beaten egg and crumbs as described. In a large heavy skillet, sauté liver strips quickly in melted fat until browned on each side. Remove to warm platter and keep hot. Heat more fat in pan, add zucchini, and sauté on each side until golden and crisp. Serve hot with liver strips. Garnish with lemon wedges.

**Fish and Zucchini Strips:** Prepare zucchini slices as described in *Broiled Liver and Zucchini Strips*. Cut fresh fish fillets (sea bass, sole, cod) in strips and season with salt and pepper. Dip in eggs and fine dry crumbs, same as zucchini. Place on well-greased cookie sheet or jellyroll pan and drizzle with oil or melted butter. Broil until crisp and golden, without turning. Or, sauté the fish and zucchini strips until golden crisp in heated butter or oil. Sprinkle with minced parsley and serve hot with lemon.

85

# Beef and Zucchini Stir-Fry

Most cooks will enjoy making this dish. Have everything prepared and laid out on a pretty tray. Then cook this delicious assortment of flavors and colors in less than 10 minutes. Great served with hot flaky rice.

3 to 4 servings

2 thin breakfast steaks or ½ pound round steak
1 onion, halved crosswise, cut in quarters
2 small zucchini, sliced diagonally
½ green pepper, cut into 1-inch squares
1 small tomato, halved crosswise, cut in wedges
1 tablespoon soy sauce
½ teaspoon sugar
2 teaspoons cornstarch
¾ cup chicken broth
3 tablespoons salad oil, divided
1 clove garlic, halved
½ teaspoon salt

On a cutting board, slice steaks (with a very sharp knife) diagonally into bacon-thin strips. Prepare onion (separate quarters into layers), zucchini, green pepper and tomato. Arrange in groups on a large platter or tray. Blend soy sauce, sugar and cornstarch and stir into chicken broth. Heat in small pan. In large heavy skillet or a Chinese wok, heat 1 tablespoon oil with garlic and salt to near smoking hot. Fish out the garlic, add steak strips, and stir-fry 2 or 3 minutes until tinged with brown. Remove to a small bowl and keep warm. Add rest of oil to pan. Heat again till near smoking and toss in the onion, pepper and zucchini. Stir-fry until all are shiny and bright, 2 or 3 minutes. Add tomato and meat strips to pan, stir, and pour in the hot broth and soy mixture. Cover and steam about 2 minutes longer, only until vegetables are crisp tender, still colorful and shapely. Serve at once.

# Mexican Zucchini Stew

Every country seems to have a favorite vegetable stew. This one is Mexico's. Tiny cubes of fresh pork flavor the colorful mixture of zucchini, onions, green peppers and tomatoes.

4 servings

*½ pound fresh lean pork*
*2 tablespoons salad oil or margarine*
*Salt and freshly ground black pepper*
*2 onions, coarsely chopped*
*1 green pepper, coarsely chopped*
*4 to 5 medium zucchini, sliced*
*1 clove garlic, chopped*
*2 ripe tomatoes, coarsely diced*

Cut pork into ½-inch cubes and blot dry with paper towels. Heat oil in heavy saucepan or stove-to-table casserole. Add pork cubes and cook slowly until browned, stirring continuously. Remove to small bowl. Season with salt and pepper. Add onions, peppers, zucchini and garlic to pan. Stir over moderate heat until onions become sort of translucent and everything is shiny and well coated. Return pork to pan and add tomatoes. Stir well, season with salt and pepper. Cover and cook gently, stirring occasionally until vegetables and pork are tender, 15 to 20 minutes.

## NOTE

Amount of pork may be increased—but somehow this amount flavors richly and seems adequate.

# Meatball Stew, Provencal

Make this sensational, budget-minded dish for a party. Savory little meatballs are simmered in fragrant *Ratatouille*, France's earthy vegetable stew of eggplant, zucchini, onions and tomatoes. It's a great meal with thick chunks of French bread, a bottle of red wine, cheese and fruit.

6 to 8 servings

*Lemon Zucchini Meatballs*
2 onions, sliced
1 eggplant, peeled, cubed, lightly floured
4 medium unpeeled zucchini, sliced, lightly floured
2 cloves garlic, chopped
4 cups coarsely diced, fresh tomatoes
   (in winter use canned)
3 to 4 tablespoons olive oil
3 to 4 tablespoons vegetable oil
2 teaspoons salt
Freshly ground black pepper to taste
1 teaspoon dried marjoram
2 teaspoons fresh minced parsley

Make meatballs as directed. Prepare vegetables ahead, if you wish, but do not flour until ready to fry. Cover and refrigerate. Heat 1 tablespoon each olive and vegetable oil in Dutch oven or heavy flameproof casserole. Add meat balls in a single layer—do not crowd. Cook until browned, shaking pan to keep balls round. Remove to bowl as they are browned. Heat 2 more tablespoons of oil in the same pan. Add onions and cook until soft. Heat more oil as needed and cook eggplant, then zucchini and garlic, until lightly browned. Stir in tomatoes and seasonings (leave parsley for later). Cover and cook gently about 20 minutes, stirring frequently to keep vegetables from sticking. Add meatballs and any juices, and stir lightly. Cover and cook gently about 20 minutes longer, until everything is tender and flavors are rich and mellow. Top with parsley.

# Lemon Zucchini Meatballs

*1½ cups soft bread crumbs*
*6 tablespoons milk*
*¼ cup grated onion*
*½ cup grated young zucchini*
*½ teaspoon grated fresh lemon peel*
*1 egg, beaten*
*1 pound ground lean beef*
*1 teaspoon salt*
*Plenty of freshly ground black pepper*

Soak bread crumbs in milk then mix thoroughly with the rest of the ingredients. Shape into 32 walnut-size balls. Lay in shallow pan, cover with foil, and refrigerate until ready to make stew.

# Josephina's Calabacita

The Mexican cook uses zucchini, or *calabacita*, in more colorful ways than any I know, except perhaps, the Italian. Josephina brought this delicious soup-stew from her native Sonora, but similar dishes are popular everywhere in Mexico. The slices of corn are messy to eat but they add flavor you won't get with cut corn. Serve in large shallow bowls with *bolillos* (crisp Mexican French rolls) and steamed rice or *frijoles refritos* (refried beans). You'll need knife, fork, and spoon and plenty of paper napkins, too.

4 big servings

*1½ pounds meaty, loin pork spareribs (often called back ribs)*
*Oil*
*Salt and freshly ground black pepper*
*1 (or more) fresh green chiles,*
*    blistered and peeled (see note)*
*    or 1 (or more) canned green chiles, seeded and chopped*
*1 large onion, chopped*
*2 cloves garlic, chopped*
*1 cup diced, peeled fresh tomatoes*
*    or 1 cup drained, canned whole tomatoes*
*½ teaspoon ground cumin*
*3 to 4 small ears of fresh corn*
*4 medium zucchini*
*Chicken broth*

Brown spare ribs slowly in a large greased, flameproof casserole or Dutch oven. Remove to bowl and season with salt and pepper. Blister chile as described below in note. Heat 2 tablespoons oil (Josephina uses lard) in same pan, add onions and chopped chile. Stir-fry until onions are soft. Add garlic, tomatoes and cumin. Stir-fry until tomatoes begin to cook, then add ribs. Mix well, cover, and cook gently about 1 hour. Husk corn, remove silks, and cut each ear into slices 1-inch thick. Remove tips from unpeeled zucchini and cut into 1-inch chunks. Add both to pot and season lightly with salt. Pour in about ¾ cup broth—dish should not be too soupy. Cover and simmer gently about 30 to 40 minutes longer, or until everything is tender and savory.

NOTE

**Blistered, Peeled Fresh Chiles:** Mexican cooks use a variety of fresh and dried chiles in their dishes and each contributes a different flavor as well as variations in hotness. The green chiles suggested here are mildly hot and marketed as California green chiles or Anaheim green chiles. If they're streaked with yellow or red, they're hotter. Lay whole chile over open gas flame and turn frequently with tongs until skin is black and charred, 3 to 4 minutes. Or place chile in broiler until skin is charred. Enclose in brown paper bag about 10 minutes, then rub off thin, bitter skin under cold running water. Remove stem, seeds, and membranes. Cut chile into strips or pieces as specified in particular recipes.

# Zucchini Meat Loaf Roast

Grated zucchini gives new flavor and moistness to this handsome loaf baked in a flat pan like a roast. Serve as you would an expensive roast, with a garland of bright vegetables around it.

6 to 8 servings

1 can (8 ounces) tomato sauce
¼ cup catsup
1½ pounds ground lean beef
1 cup grated zucchini (2 medium)
½ medium onion, grated
1 small clove garlic, minced
1 teaspoon salt
1 egg
1 teaspoon Worcestershire sauce
½ cup dry bread crumbs
Freshly ground black pepper

Mix tomato sauce and catsup. Combine all ingredients in a large bowl, leaving out ½ cup tomato sauce mixture for top. Mix ingredients thoroughly with hands, then shape into a thick oval loaf in a shallow baking pan. Make 4 diagonal slashes across top with back of table knife and spread reserved tomato sauce mixture over top of loaf. Bake at 350°F. 1 hour and 15 to 20 minutes, until browned and glazed. Let stand 10 minutes before removing to platter. Surround with *French Glazed Carrots* (see index), tiny new potatoes and green beans.

**VARIATION**

Substitute 1 cup grated raw carrot for the zucchini.

# Zucchini Mozzarella, Alfonse

Here's a fast, quick way to copy a favorite Italian specialty featured for luncheon at a restaurant in my neighborhood. Alfonse chefs cover sautéed zucchini or eggplant—depending on which is better in the market—with their own tomato or meat sauce, mozzarella, sliced avocado and bacon. It's marvelous—and a substantial meal. I've simplified their elaborate preparation for this home recipe.

*4 big servings*

*1 package spaghetti sauce mix*
*1 (8 ounce) can tomato sauce*
*Olive or vegetable oil*
*4 large zucchini*
*Salt*
*Pepper*
*Flour*
*1 cup coarsely shredded or sliced mozzarella cheese*
*Grated Parmesan cheese*
*4 slices lean bacon*

Prepare spaghetti sauce mix by package directions with tomato sauce and 2 tablespoons olive oil. While it simmers, remove tips from zucchini, halve them crosswise, then slice each lengthwise into about 3 flat slices. Sprinkle with salt and pepper, and roll in flour. Brown lightly in a film of hot oil and drain on paper towels. Place 1-layer deep in large shallow baking dish—or individual dishes as used by Alfonse. Cover zucchini with mozzarella cheese. Top with spaghetti sauce and sprinkle with 2 to 3 tablespoons grated Parmesan. Bake at 350°F. about 30 minutes, until bubbly hot. Meanwhile cook bacon until nearly crisp. Drain and place on top of dish (Alfonse also presses slices of avocado into the sauce and then tops with bacon). Run under broiler a few minutes to glaze and to crisp the bacon.

# Moussaka

This popular meat and vegetable casserole with puffy custard topping is said to have originated in Turkey, but is served throughout Southeastern Europe. Generally made with eggplant, it may be done with potatoes, zucchini, artichokes, etc. Zucchini makes a lighter, easier dish.

8 servings

4 medium to large zucchini (7 to 8 inches long)
Flour
Olive or vegetable oil
1½ cups chopped onion
½ pound ground lean beef
½ pound ground lean lamb
1 clove garlic, minced
2 tablespoons chopped parsley
Pinch of cinnamon
1 bay leaf, crumbled
¼ teaspoon oregano
¼ teaspoon fennel seeds
Salt and pepper to taste
1 can (8 ounces) tomato sauce
½ cup water or broth
¼ cup coarse dry bread crumbs
Creamy Topping
½ cup grated Parmesan cheese

Halve unpeeled zucchini crosswise and cut each into about 3 lengthwise slices. Flour lightly. Heat 2 tablespoons oil in large heavy skillet, add zucchini, and brown lightly. Add more oil if needed. Drain on paper towels. Heat 2 tablespoons oil in the same pan, add onions, and cook until soft. Crumble in meat and cook and stir until lightly browned. Add garlic, parsley, seasonings, tomato sauce and water or broth. Mix

94

well, lower heat, and cook gently until sauce has cooked down and thickened, about 30 minutes. Stir frequently. Make Creamy Topping. Grease a large, shallow 2-quart baking dish and put in half the zucchini slices. Sprinkle with salt, pepper and half the crumbs. Cover with meat sauce, crumbs and zucchini. Spread Creamy Topping evenly over all and sprinkle with Parmesan. Bake at 350°F. 45 minutes to 1 hour. Remove from oven and let casserole stand about 15 minutes before serving. Cut into squares.

## Creamy Topping

*2 tablespoons butter or margarine*
*2 tablespoons flour*
*2 cups milk*
*½ teaspoon salt*
*Pinch of nutmeg*
*2 egg yolks*

Melt butter in small heavy saucepan and blend in flour. Cook and stir without browning, about 2 minutes. Add milk and stir over low heat until sauce boils and thickens. Season with salt and nutmeg. Beat egg yolks with wire whisk and stir in a little of the sauce. Stir this back into saucepan and stir sauce over low heat about ½ minute.

# Zucchini Lasagne

Avid pasta fans may shake their heads at a lasagne without noodles. Nevertheless, a well-seasoned lasagne sauce baked over succulent zucchini strips, with typical Italian cheeses, makes a marvelous dish—much lighter than the original.

6 man-size servings

1 small onion, chopped
2 tablespoons olive or vegetable oil
½ pound ground lean beef
¼ pound ground lean pork
  or mild sausage
2 cloves garlic, minced
½ teaspoon each oregano
  and sweet basil
Pinch of allspice
Pinch of sugar
1 teaspoon salt

Freshly ground black pepper
1 can (1 pound) tomatoes
1 can (6 ounces) tomato paste
1 cup beef stock, bouillon or water
4 medium-large zucchini (can be
  fat, more mature zucchini,
  8 inches long)
¼ cup dry bread crumbs
4 ounces (1 cup) coarsely shredded
  mozzarella cheese
8 ounces (1 cup) ricotta cheese
½ cup grated Parmesan cheese

In heavy saucepan, cook onion in oil until soft. Add meats and garlic and cook, stirring continuously, until meat is lightly browned and crumbly. Add seasonings, tomatoes, paste, and stock. Mix well and simmer over low heat until sauce is thick and savory, about 1 hour. Stir occasionally. Check seasonings when sauce is finished. Steam unpeeled zucchini, covered, in 1 inch of boiling water, with ½ teaspoon salt, for 5 to 7 minutes only. Rinse quickly in cold water to stop cooking. Cut each lengthwise into slices about ¼-inch thick. Oil a large, shallow casserole and sprinkle with 2 tablespoons crumbs. Lay half the zucchini in the dish, top with half the sauce and mozzarella and all the ricotta, crumbled. Sprinkle with crumbs and fill dish with rest of zucchini and sauce. Top with mozzarella and Parmesan. Bake at 350°F. 45 minutes to 1 hour.

# Pastitsio

This thrifty Greek macaroni casserole or pie has the same custardy topping usually baked on Moussaka. A good dish for a buffet supper or outdoor party, it can be served for a luncheon too.

8 to 10 servings

*Meat Sauce for Moussaka (see p. 94)*
*(see p. 94)*
*using ¾ pound each*
*gound beef and ground lamb and*
*1 cup beef bouillon instead of ½ cup water or broth*
*Creamy Topping (see preceding recipe), using*
*3 tablespoons butter or margarine*
*3 tablespoons flour*
*3 cups milk*
*¾ teaspoon salt*
*Pinch of nutmeg*
*3 egg yolks*
*2 small zucchini, finely diced*
*1 tablespoon olive oil*
*½ pound small elbow macaroni*
*Salt*
*½ cup plus 2 tablespoons grated Parmesan cheese*

🍲 Make meat sauce as described in *Moussaka* recipe increasing meat amounts as indicated above. Make *Creamy Topping* as described, increasing amounts as indicated. Sauté zucchini lightly in oil for about 1 minute. Cook macaroni in boiling salted water until tender but still *al dente*. Drain in colander and shake out moisture. Mix with zucchini and ½ cup *Creamy Topping*. Butter a large shallow casserole (2½-quart size) and put in a layer of half the macaroni, half the meat sauce, sprinkle with 2 tablespoons grated Parmesan cheese. Top with second layer of macaroni and meat sauce. Spread *Creamy Topping* evenly over all and sprinkle with ½ cup grated Parmesan cheese. Bake at 350°F. about 45 minutes to 1 hour, or until sauce is puffed and flecked with brown. Remove from oven and let stand about 15 minutes. Cut into squares.

# Zucchini Sausage Pie

Zucchini topped with an unusual sausage mixture makes a delicious and thrifty dish for supper or a luncheon with salad and fresh fruit.

6 servings

1 pound bulk pork sausage
1 large onion, chopped
½ cup fine, dry bread crumbs
½ cup 100% bran cereal
½ teaspoon dried marjoram
½ teaspoon dried oregano leaves, crushed
2 tablespoons tomato paste
½ cup sour cream
6 medium-small zucchini (about 6 inches long)
Salt and freshly ground black pepper
⅓ cup grated Parmesan cheese
4 ounces Monterey Jack cheese, coarsely shredded

Crumble sausage into a heavy skillet. Cook and stir with a wooden spoon until browned. Drain off fat, saving 2 tablespoons. In the same pan, cook onion in 2 tablespoons of drippings until soft. Mix with sausage, bread crumbs, bran, herbs, tomato paste and sour cream. Wash zucchini and steam whole, unpeeled, in tightly covered pan in about ½ cup boiling salted water. Cook only 3 to 5 minutes (you cook them more later). Drain and slice lengthwise into flat slices about ⅛-inch thick. Line a shallow oblong baking dish with half the slices, sprinkle with salt and pepper and half the Parmesan. Spread with sausage mixture and top with the rest of the zucchini. Repeat with salt, pepper and Parmesan. Cover with foil and bake at 350°F. about 30 minutes. Uncover and top with Jack cheese. Bake 10 minutes longer, or until cheese melts and is flecked with brown. Cut in squares to serve.

# Pasta with Zucchini

You can make this fresh light sauce while your pasta boils, if you have the dicing and chopping done ahead. It's a great dish for an impromptu supper or patio luncheon.

4 servings

3 cups finely diced, unpeeled young zucchini (3 to 4 medium)
3 finely chopped green onions and bits of tops
3 cups chopped, peeled fresh tomatoes (or lightly drained canned sliced baby tomatoes)
1 large clove garlic, minced
2 tablespoons chopped fresh parsley
1 can (2 ounces) anchovy fillets, chopped
½ cup freshly grated Parmesan cheese
Salt
3 tablespoons butter or margarine
1 tablespoon olive oil
Freshly ground black pepper
1 pound linguine, spaghettini, or other small pasta

Prepare all the vegetables, chop the anchovies, and grate the cheese before you start to cook. Put on large pot of salted water for pasta and heat to boiling. In heavy saucepan, heat 3 tablespoons butter and the olive oil. Add zucchini, green onion and anchovies. Stir-fry until slightly softened, 2 or 3 minutes. Add tomatoes, garlic and parsley. Stir until everything is shiny. Cook slowly, stirring frequently a few more minutes. Everything should be just barely tender and still colorful. Season with pepper—no salt is needed. Cook pasta in the boiling water until *al dente*, drain into a colander, and shake out the moisture. Put butter in the hot pasta cooking pot and put pasta back in it. Toss pasta with butter and half the cheese. Pour on the sauce and toss again, lightly, until well mixed. Serve on warm plates and sprinkle with rest of cheese.

# Lamb Shanks, Rosemary

Lamb shoulder chops work equally well in this robust dish. (The chops will be done in an hour or so.) Serve with French bread and a light salad.

4 servings

4 lamb shanks (uncracked at joints, if possible)
Salt and freshly ground black pepper
Vegetable oil
1 onion, finely chopped
1 clove garlic, chopped
2 tablespoons chopped parsley
¾ cup bouillon or light, dry red wine
1 teaspoon crumbled dried rosemary
12 small carrots, scraped

Rub lamb shanks with salt and pepper and brown lightly in a teaspoon or two of oil in a flameproof casserole or a heavy skillet. (Transfer meat to an oven casserole if skillet is used for browning.) Cook onion in 1 tablespoon oil until soft, 3 to 5 minutes. Stir in garlic and parsley, cook 1 minute longer. Add bouillon (or wine) and rosemary, heat to boiling, and pour over meat. Cover tightly and braise in moderately slow oven (325°F.) 1½ hours. Skim fat from pan and add carrots. Turn them to coat evenly with pan sauce. Cook 45 minutes to 1 hour longer, until carrots are tender.

# Sneaky Burgers

A number of our California restaurants that cater to diet-conscious movie and T.V. personalities feature hamburgers laced with all sorts of raw vegetables. One night I sneaked some grated carrots into our hamburgers and the light, moist open-textured hamburgers were an instant hit. Try these and you'll see what I mean.

4 servings

1 pound ground lean chuck beef
4 tablespoons grated raw carrot
2 to 4 tablespoons finely chopped tomato
2 tablespoons finely chopped onion
1 tablespoon chopped parsley
Salt
Pepper
Butter or margarine
Hamburger buns, kaiser rolls, French bread or pita

Lightly work into the meat with your fingers or a fork, the carrots, tomato, onion and parsley. Season with salt and pepper. Shape into 4 patties. Cook quickly on a lightly oiled hot griddle until browned on each side and juicy moist inside. Serve at once on buttered hamburger buns, kaiser rolls, French bread or tucked into the pocket of pita with some of those *Fabulous Zucchini French Fries* (see index).

# Carrots in Stews, Worldwide

Carrots lend their sweet flavor and bright color to stews and hearty one-dish meals the world over. We can't imagine France's savory *pot au feu* of boiled beef and chicken without carrots among the seasoning vegetables, as well as the carrots that garnish the finished dish. Nor can we imagine Ireland's simple layered stew of lamb and vegetables, without carrots. The Netherlands' *hutspot*, or hodge-podge, needs carrots to make it complete as do Spain's and Latin America's *pucheros* and *cocidas*, those marvelous soup-stews of beans, meats, and vegetables. Our own New England Boiled Dinner wouldn't be the same without the brightness of carrots.

# Beef en Daube

Here is a delicious example of carrots in a cosmopolitan stew! The secret of the deep, rich, almost voluptuous flavor is to marinate the meat in wine with herbs and vegetables, then oven-braise very slowly in a covered casserole. This process gives an entirely different flavor than you get from a stew simmered on top of the stove. The name *daube* comes from *daubière*, a covered casserole, often made of stoneware or earthenware, used in France for this and similar braised dishes. If you own one of the popular slow cookers, cook the *daube* in it for 6 hours or so. Serve with French bread, tiny boiled potatoes or rice.

6 servings

*2 slices bacon, cut in pieces*
*2½ pounds boneless beef chuck, cut in 2-inch cubes*
*2 cups sliced onions (see note)*
*2 cups sliced, scraped carrots (about 6 medium)—see note*
*1 clove garlic, chopped*
*1 bay leaf, broken or crumbled*
*½ teaspoon dried marjoram leaves*

1 teaspoon salt
Freshly ground black pepper
1 3-inch strip of orange peel stuck with 2 whole cloves
1 cup dry red wine
Flour
1 tablespoon vegetable oil
1½ cups beef stock (or canned bouillon or bouillon cubes)
Minced parsley

Cover bacon with cold water and simmer 5 to 10 minutes. Drain and place in large bowl with meat, vegetables, seasonings and wine. Cover and marinate several hours, or overnight in the refrigerator. Remove meat from marinade, blot dry with paper towels, and roll in flour to coat lightly. Heat oil in heavy skillet and brown meat along with the strip of orange peel and cloves. Remove to a large 3- or 4-quart casserole and add the orange peel and all the marinating ingredients. Pour in meat stock to nearly cover meat. Cover tightly and braise in moderately slow oven (325°F.) about 3 hours, or until very tender. If liquid has not cooked down enough to make a slightly thickened sauce, tilt casserole and drain liquid into a saucepan. Skim off excess fat. Moisten a little cornstarch to a paste with cold water and stir into boiling sauce (allow 2 teaspoons cornstarch for each cup of pan liquid). Stir over medium heat until sauce is bubbling, smooth and lightly thickened. Taste, and adjust seasonings. Return to casserole and mix gently. Sprinkle with minced parsley and serve from dish.

### NOTE

If you wish, reduce onions and carrots for marinade to 1 cup each. Add to casserole, for the last hour of cooking, a dozen or so small whole carrots, scraped, and a dozen small boiling onions.

# Wine Country Chicken Stew

This homey chicken stew picks up a bit of French finesse in its silky finishing sauce. Tiny carrots and onions are beautiful and tasty with it. Rice, noodles, hot biscuits or French bread are good served with this.

4 servings

*1 roaster or chicken fryer (about 3 pounds), disjointed*
*Lemon juice*
*Salt and freshly ground black pepper*
*Flour*
*Light vegetable oil*
*2 cups water*
*1 cup dry white table wine*
*Thick slice onion stuck with 2 cloves*
*2 or 3 carrot slices*
*1 bay leaf*
*½ teaspoon dried marjoram crumbled*
*1 dozen small whole onions, peeled*
*16 to 20 tiny carrots (or small carrots*
*    cut in 3-inch pieces)*
*¼ cup half-and-half (milk and cream)*
*1 egg yolk*
*Minced parsley*

Sprinkle chicken with lemon juice and season with salt and pepper. Dust with flour, shake off excess, and brown chicken lightly in about 1 tablespoon light vegetable oil. Transfer to deep kettle or flameproof casserole and add water, wine, onion slice with cloves, carrot slices, bay leaf, marjoram and about ½ teaspoon salt. Cover and simmer gently until chicken is tender, 30 to 45 minutes. Remove chicken to a warm bowl, cover, and keep warm. Parboil onions in boiling salted water 5 minutes and add to broth along with carrots. Cover and cook until both are tender, 20 to 25 minutes. Scoop out seasoning vegetables if you can, but it's not too important. Skim fat from top of broth. Gradually blend 2 tablespoons flour into the half-and-half to form a smooth creamy paste. Blend in egg yolk. Stir 2 or 3 spoonfuls of hot broth into this, then stir mixture back into hot broth. Stir with whisk over low heat until sauce thickens, about 2 minutes. Add 1 teaspoon (or to taste) fresh lemon juice and more salt, if needed. Return chicken to sauce and heat for a few moments, but do not boil. Serve from casserole or deep serving dish. Sprinkle with parsley.

## NOTE

A stewing chicken is cheaper and requires 2½ to 3 hours simmering time. Chicken pieces are not as meaty, but the broth and finished sauce will be very rich and flavorful.

# Student's Stew

Students are not the only ones who will enjoy this easy, one-pot meal. But it has long been a favorite with the thrifty students in the Latin Quarter of Paris. Tastes great with a glass of red wine and a leafy salad.

4 to 6 servings

*4 slices of lean bacon*
*1½ pounds chuck or round steak*
*Flour*
*Salt and pepper*
*Pinch of thyme*
*1 bay leaf*
*3 onions, sliced*
*6 medium carrots, scraped, halved*
  *cut in 4-inch pieces*
*3 to 4 medium boiling potatoes*
*1 cup water*

Cut bacon slices in half and put 2 of them in the bottom of a large heavy pot or Dutch oven. Cut steak at an angle across grain into ½-inch strips about 3 inches long. Roll in flour and spread half of the steak strips over the bacon. Season well with salt and pepper, thyme and the bay leaf, crumbled. Cover with onions and carrots, season, and add the rest of the meat. Season that and cover with potatoes, peeled and sliced. Season potatoes with salt and pepper and cover with the rest of the bacon. Cover tightly and set over moderate heat until bacon starts to cook. Pour in 1 cup water, cover again, and turn heat low. Cook gently until everything is tender and savory, about 1½ hours.

# 5

# Cool Salads, Relishes, and Pickles

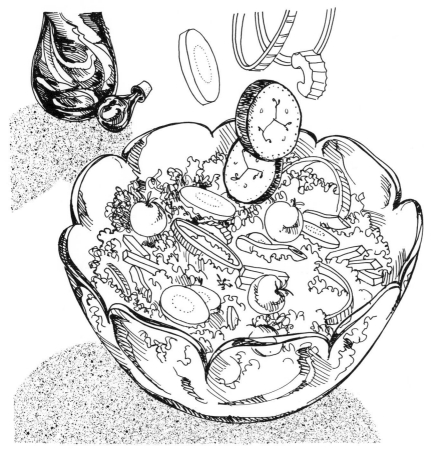

# Zucchini Tomato Salad

Thickly sliced tomatoes covered with marinated raw zucchini make a salad as bright and flavorful as a summer garden.

6 servings

3 medium zucchini (6 inches long
   no thicker than 1 inch)
4 or 5 green onions and parts of tops, sliced
1 clove garlic, crushed
½ teaspoon salt
3 tablespoons wine vinegar
½ cup salad oil
1 tablespoon chopped fresh sweet basil
   or 1 teaspoon dried
Freshly ground black pepper
3 or 4 red-ripe tomatoes
2 tablespoons minced fresh parsley

Remove tips from unpeeled zucchini and slice thinly into bowl. Add green onions. Crush garlic with salt and blend in vinegar, salad oil, and basil. Pour over vegetables. Mix well and add pepper to taste. Cover and chill. At serving time, line a platter with sliced tomatoes. Season lightly with salt and pepper and top with zucchini, spooning some of the marinade over tomatoes. Sprinkle everything with parsley. Serve very cold.

# Iced Dill Zucchini

Serve this as salad with lettuce and trimmings or without the embellishments as a relish.

4 to 6 servings

2 pounds medium zucchini
Salt
1 cup peeled, cooked small shrimp (optional)
1 cup vinegar
1 large clove garlic, minced
1 bay leaf, crumbled
2 teaspoons dill seeds
¼ cup brown sugar
1 crisp white onion
Lettuce leaves or shredded iceberg lettuce
Sour cream, mayonnaise, or Buttermilk Dressing
Chopped fresh dill or parsley

Cut unpeeled zucchini crosswise on a slant into longish ovals about ½ inch thick. Cook gently in 2 cups boiling water with about 1 teaspoon salt until crisp tender, 4 to 5 minutes. Drain cooking liquid and save it. Place zucchini in a bowl and add shrimp if you're in the money. Combine vinegar with cooking liquid, garlic, bay leaf, dill seeds and brown sugar. Simmer 6 to 10 minutes and pour over zucchini. Add onion, thinly sliced and separated into rings. Cover and chill overnight or several days. Serve as salad in crisp lettuce leaves or in nests of shredded iceberg lettuce. Drizzle some of the pickle liquid over salad as a light dressing. If you want a heavier dressing, top with a little sour cream, mayonnaise or the *Buttermilk Dressing*, p. 122. Sprinkle with fresh dill or parsley.

# Zucchini Salad Bowl

Experience a new taste with thin slices of fresh young zucchini in your favorite salad bowl. This is a popular combination at our house.

4 to 6 servings

*4 cups bite-size pieces romaine lettuce*
*5 or 6 sprigs chicory (curly endive),*
*   coarsely chopped*
*½ of a sweet red onion*
*2 small zucchini, unpeeled*
*1 soft-ripe avocado*
*Salt and freshly ground black pepper*
*Lemon Vinaigrette (p. 116)*
*Chopped fresh basil*
*1 cup cherry tomatoes*

Wash and prepare greens. Dry well and roll in a towel to chill. Chill onion and zucchini. Put greens in bottom of salad bowl. Slice onion thinly and separate into rings. Add to greens. Tip and slice zucchini thinly onto greens. Cut avocado into halves, twist to separate. Remove skin and seed, and dice avocado into the salad bowl. Season with salt and pepper. Season *Lemon Vinaigrette* with fresh basil to taste. Toss salad gently with about 4 tablespoons of the dressing, or enough to coat everything well but not make it soggy. Top with halved cherry tomatoes, and sprinkle lightly with salt and pepper.

# Mushroom and Zucchini Salad

For this salad use very young tender zucchini and crisp fresh mushrooms. The bit of cream in the dressing gives a subtle flavor and texture that's appealing with these two delicately flavored vegetables.

6 servings

2 cups sliced tender young zucchini (3 or 4 small)
4 tablespoons Oil and Vinegar Dressing (p. 117)
½ pound fresh mushrooms
1 tablespoon fresh lemon juice
2 tablespoons minced parsley
1 clove garlic, minced (optional)
Romaine and Boston or Bibb lettuce
2 tablespoons heavy cream
2 teaspoons Dijon mustard
Salt
Freshly ground black pepper
2 tablespoons chopped, lightly toasted walnuts

Slice enough zucchini very thinly to measure 2 cups and pour over them *Oil and Vinegar Dressing*. Wipe mushrooms with damp paper towels and trim off stems. Slice mushrooms lengthwise, (you should have 2 cups slices) and mix lightly with lemon juice to coat evenly. Add to zucchini. Stir in parsley and the extra clove of garlic if you like a more garlicky dressing. Cover and marinate 1 hour. Shake or stir occasionally. Wash and dry enough romaine and Boston or Bibb lettuce for 6 servings. Roll in towel to chill. At serving time put greens in salad bowl. Remove vegetables from dressing and place on top. Add heavy cream and Dijon mustard to dressing, mix well and add to salad. Toss lightly and season with salt and a little freshly ground pepper. Top with lightly toasted walnuts. Serve at once.

# Zucchini à la Russe

Everything dressed with sour cream we tend to dub Russian or a la Russe, so I'm guilty here too. Similar, and yet different from cucumbers in sour cream this is a delicious change for those who can't eat cucumbers. Serve as a salad or a relish.

4 to 6 servings

*4 tender young zucchini*
*Salt*
*1 sweet white or red onion*
*1 cup (or more) sour cream*
*1 tablespoon chopped fresh dill*
   *(or 1 teaspoon dried)*
*Few snips fresh or a pinch of dried tarragon*
*Freshly ground black pepper*

Remove tips and slice zucchini paper thin. Sprinkle with salt and put in strainer to drain for about 30 minutes. Blot zucchini dry with paper towels and layer in pretty glass bowl with thinly sliced onion separated into rings. Mix sour cream with dill and tarragon, a little black pepper if you wish. Pour over vegetables, cover with foil and chill. Mix gently and sprinkle with more dill or chopped parsley.

# Ratatouille

From Provence in south France, this is one of the great vegetable dishes of all time. It can be served hot, but it is even better cold. Perfect with grilled meats, it can also go it alone with crusty bread, cheese, and fruit. Or tuck it into the pocket of pita bread for a marvelous out-of-hand meal.

6 to 8 servings

*1 small eggplant (about 1 pound)*
*4 to 5 medium zucchini (about 1 pound)*
*Salt*
*2 onions, halved and sliced*
*1 green and 1 red bell pepper, seeded, cut in strips*
*4 large tomatoes, skinned and diced (about 4 cups)*
*½ cup olive or vegetable oil*
*2 cloves garlic, chopped*
*½ teaspoon leaf thyme, crumbled*
*1 teaspoon dried marjoram, crumbled*
*Freshly ground black pepper*
*2 tablespoons chopped fresh parsley*
*Lemon wedges*
*Black olives*

Cut unpeeled eggplant into ¾-inch chunks. Slice unpeeled zucchini into ½-inch slices. Place both in colander and sprinkle with salt to draw out excess moisture. Let stand at least 30 minutes while you prepare other vegetables. Heat half the oil in large heavy skillet or flameproof casserole. Add onion and peppers and cook, stirring often, until soft but not browned. Scoop into a bowl. Heat rest of oil in the same pan. Press moisture out of eggplant and zucchini and add them to oil with garlic. Cook and stir until they are beginning to soften, about 5 minutes. Return onions and peppers to pan, add tomatoes and herbs. Stir until tomatoes begin to cook, then season with salt and pepper to taste. Lower heat, cover, and simmer until vegetables are tender but still shapely, 30 to 45 minutes. Stir frequently. Add parsley and serve hot or chill overnight and serve cold with lemon wedges and black olives.

# Zucchini Carrot Vinaigrette

The colors and flavors of the two vegetables contrast handsomely here. Cook them separately for best results.

6 to 8 servings

6 medium zucchini (6 inches long)
Salt
4 to 6 young carrots (6 inches long)
Sugar
Lemon Vinaigrette
Lettuce leaves or chicory
2 tablespoons finely chopped parsley
2 tablespoons finely chopped green onion
1 teaspoon coarsely grated lemon peel
Cherry tomatoes

Trim tips from zucchini, cut into halves lengthwise, then into thin sticks. Cook covered in ½ cup boiling water with ½ teaspoon salt 2 to 3 minutes only. Drain. Scrape carrots, halve lengthwise and cut into thin sticks. Cook covered in ½ inch boiling water with ¼ teaspoon each salt and sugar, 5 to 6 minutes. Drain. Lay both vegetables in shallow dish (keep separate) and drizzle with several spoonfuls of *Lemon Vinaigrette*. Cover and chill several hours or overnight. Remove vegetables from marinade with slotted spoon and pile symmetrically in a shallow glass bowl lined with small lettuce leaves or chicory. Top with parsley, onions and lemon peel. Add more vinaigrette to dress salad nicely. Rim dish with halved cherry tomatoes.

# Lemon Vinaigrette

1 small clove garlic                                    ½ cup
½ teaspoon salt
¼ teaspoon dry mustard
1 tablespoon red wine vinegar
1 tablespoon fresh lemon juice
6 tablespoons olive and vegetable oil mixed
Freshly ground black pepper
1 tablespoon chopped fresh or
    1 teaspoon dried tarragon leaves

Crush to a paste the garlic, salt and mustard. With wire whisk, blend in wine vinegar and lemon juice. Slowly whisk in salad oil. Use some olive oil for flavor but supplement with safflower, corn or peanut oil, if you wish. Whisk until dressing is smooth and slightly thickened. Season with freshly ground pepper and 1 tablespoon chopped fresh tarragon (or 1 teaspoon dried tarragon leaves).

SEE ALSO *Antipasto Zucchini* (p. 47)
    *Antipasto Carrots* (p. 47)

# Shredded Carrot Salad

Simplest and freshest tasting of all carrot salads. Shred tender young carrots into long slender shreds. Shred enough celery hearts or the tender heart of a fennel bulb into thin slivers to measure half as much as carrots. Combine and toss lightly with *Lemon Vinaigrette*. Chill and heap into frilly lettuce leaves. Finely chop a few of the leafy green tops from fennel (or use parsley) and sprinkle over salad.

## VARIATION

**Mystery Carrot Salad:** Chill overnight finely shredded raw carrots in orange juice with plenty of grated orange peel. Tastes exotic and needs no other dressing.

# Spinach Salad, Italian Style

The Italians make spinach salad without bacon—although bacon can be sprinkled on top, if you wish. The crunch is provided by shredded carrot, celery, red onion and finnochio (the French call it fennel).

4 to 6 servings

*3 to 4 cups chopped raw spinach*
*1 cup thinly sliced celery hearts*
*1 cup shredded young carrots*
*1 cup thinly sliced finocchio (sweet anise or fennel)*
*½ cup thin red onion slices*
*Oil and Vinegar Dressing*

Cut stems from fresh young spinach and wash leaves through several waters. Blot dry with paper towels and chop coarsely. Slice celery hearts and shred scraped carrots. Slice the inner white bulb of finocchio thinly, then separate into slivers. Cut onion slices in half and separate into slivers. Put vegetables in salad bowl and toss with 3 or 4 spoonfuls of *Oil and Vinegar Dressing*. Season with salt and freshly ground black pepper.

## Oil and Vinegar Dressing
1 cup

*1 clove garlic*
*¾ teaspoon salt*
*1 teaspoon Dijon mustard*
*¼ cup red wine vinegar*
*¾ cup olive and vegetable oil, mixed*
*Freshly ground black pepper*
*Herbs ad lib, depending on salad*

Crush garlic in the salt with mustard. With wire whisk blend in vinegar, then slowly whisk in salad oil. Whisk until blended and slightly thickened. Add pepper and herbs as desired.

117

# Green and Gold Salad

A pretty make-ahead salad of cooked green beans and young carrots accented with crisp red onion, radishes and bacon bits. Look for the tiny, tiny carrots and skinny green beans for this, and cook them separately to enhance their individual flavors.

6 servings

1 pound tender, young green beans
Salt
1 pound tiny carrots (or 3-inch sticks
   from longer carrots)
Sugar
1 small red onion, thinly sliced, separated into rings
2 tablespoons chopped parsley
Oil and Vinegar Dressing (preceding recipe)
Crisp chilled salad greens
1 tablespoon chopped fresh dill or
   fennel tops (optional)
¼ cup sliced radishes
¼ cup crisp-cooked bacon bits
Freshly ground black pepper

Remove tips and strings from beans, cut in half, and cook in boiling salted water until crisp-tender, 10 to 12 minutes. Blanch quickly in cold water to stop cooking. Drain. At same time, put scraped carrots in 1 cup boiling water with ½ teaspoon each salt and sugar. Cover, and cook about 5 minutes for sticks, 8 to 10 minutes for whole carrots. Drain and combine with beans, onion rings and 1 tablespoon parsley. Pour over them 4 to 5 tablespoons Oil and Vinegar Dressing. Mix gently and chill. At serving time, put a base of crisp dry salad greens in bowl—you don't need a lot since this is a bean and carrot salad. Add marinated vegetables, rest of parsley, the dill or fennel and radishes. Toss to mix well, adding more dressing if needed. Season with salt and pepper, top with bacon bits. Serve at once.

# Carrot Walnut Salad

The secret of this simple but impressive salad or marinated cooked vegetable is to toss the carrots in the herbs and dressing while they're hot. When ready to serve, top with the crisp, toasted walnuts. It's convenient and pretty for a buffet.

4 to 6 servings

4 cups tiny carrots (or 4-inch sticks
   from longer young carrots)
Salt
Sugar
1 tablespoon chopped fresh tarragon (or 1 teaspoon dried)
1 tablespoon finely chopped parsley
2 tablespoons chopped green onions
1 small clove garlic, crushed
2 tablespoons dry white wine
6 tablespoons olive or vegetable oil
1 tablespoon wine vinegar
1 tablespoon lemon juice
Freshly ground black pepper
½ cup walnut halves
Watercress
Lemon slices

Put carrots in heavy saucepan with 1 inch boiling water and ½ teaspoon each salt and sugar. Cover and cook gently until crunchy-tender, about 5 minutes for the sticks, a few minutes longer for the whole carrots. While hot, drain and sprinkle with herbs, onion, garlic and wine. Toss with oil, then the vinegar and lemon mixed. There should be just enough marinade to coat and season carrots well but not make them soggy. Season with a little salt, if needed, and a few grindings of pepper. Cover and chill. Blanch walnuts in boiling water for 2 minutes. Drain and slip off skins. Blot dry. Toast lightly in a skillet in a teaspoon or two of butter or oil, or on a cookie sheet in 325°F. oven for about 10 minutes. Turn marinated carrots into a pretty glass bowl rimmed with sprays of watercress. Top with walnut halves and thin slices of lemon, cut in half.

119

A trio of oldies but goodies that never seem to lose their appeal.

# Carrot Ambrosia Salad

4 to 5 servings

3 cups shredded raw carrots
1 cup orange slices, cut in wedges
¼ cup slivered dates or seedless raisins
1 cup flaked coconut
½ cup sour cream
1 to 2 tablespoons honey
Dash of ground ginger
Dash of salt
Lettuce leaves

Combine carrots with orange pieces, dates or raisins and coconut. Blend sour cream and honey, to taste, with the ginger and salt. Pour over salad and toss gently to mix. Chill and serve on lettuce leaves.

# Carrot Slaw

4 servings

2 cups shredded young green cabbage
1 cup shredded raw carrots
2 finely chopped green onions
Salt
Pepper
Buttermilk Dressing (see index)
2 teaspoons sugar
1 teaspoon Dijon-style mustard
Chopped salted nuts (any kind)

Mix cabbage with carrots and onion. Season with salt and pepper, and toss with about ⅓ cup *Buttermilk Dressing* flavored with sugar and mustard. Chill. Top with chopped, salted nuts when ready to serve.

*Variations* seem infinite. Add ½ cup pineapple chunks, thin slivers of unpeeled red apple, sliced stuffed or ripe olives, capers, or a handful of bean sprouts. Vary the dressing with curry powder, caraway seeds, dill or celery seeds.

# Old-Timer Perfection Salad

6 servings

*1 package (3 ounces) lemon or lime flavor gelatin*
*1 cup boiling water*
*¾ cup cold water*
*Salt*
*2 tablespoons vinegar*
*¾ cup shredded green cabbage*
*¾ cup shredded raw carrots*
*¼ cup diced green bell pepper*
*2 tablespoons diced pimiento*
*1 tablespoon chopped chives*
*Lettuce leaves*
*Buttermilk Dressing (see index)*
*(or mayonnaise with yogurt or sour cream)*
*Honey*

Dissolve gelatin in boiling water and blend in cold water, salt to taste, and vinegar. Chill until syrupy thick. Have ready shredded cabbage, carrots, bell pepper, pimiento and chives. Fold into thickened gelatin and turn into an 8-inch square pan. Chill firm. Cut into oblongs and serve on lettuce leaves. *Buttermilk Dressing* lightly sweetened with honey is nice with this. Another good dressing is mayonnaise mixed with an equal amount of yogurt or sour cream and lightly sweetened. *Vary* with sliced stuffed olives in place of the green pepper and a little grated onion for the chives.

# Salad of the Desert

Years ago I enjoyed this salad on a scorching day in California's low desert near Indio. I've never forgotten the crunch of the raw carrots and toasted almonds, the cool cottage cheese and juicy desert fruits around it.

Makes 2 full-meal luncheon salads

*2 tender small carrots, to be grated*
*10 fresh dates*
*1½ cups small curd cottage cheese*
*Crisp lettuce, shredded*
*1 cup fresh grapefruit sections, chilled*
*1 cup fresh orange sections, chilled*
*2 tablespoons chopped toasted almonds*
*Thin carrot sticks, chilled*
*French Dressing, or Buttermilk Dressing*

Grate carrots and slice half a dozen dates. Stir lightly into cottage cheese. Mound in center of crisp shredded lettuce on 2 salad plates. Surround with a wreath of ice cold grapefruit and orange sections. Top cheese with crisply toasted almonds. Decorate each plate with a handful of crisp thin carrot sticks and a couple of plump dates. You don't need a dressing with all this—but a lemony French dressing (see index for *Lemon Vinaigrette*) of the zingy *Buttermilk Dressing* below would be good.

## Buttermilk Dressing

Buttermilk gives a fresh flavor, cuts down on calories. Combine equal parts buttermilk and mayonnaise and stir until smooth and creamy. Add herbs, garlic, parsley, chives or other seasoning, ad lib—but it tastes good even without herbs.

# Relishes and Pickles

"Putting up pickles and relishes" need not be a big, hot summer chore that must be done when pickling cucumbers, tiny onions, tomatoes and such are at their abundant best. Most of the pickles and relishes suggested here can be made anytime of the year, to add a spicy zest to your meals. Because zucchini has a soft texture and the ability to absorb flavors readily, these pickles can be made today and enjoyed 2 or 3 days later. Make them in small batches along with your regular cooking and keep in the refrigerator to enjoy at will.

# Pickled Vegetables Picante

A titillating mixture of pickled vegetables that's ideal for an outdoor feast. You've likely seen similar combinations labelled Hot Chile Mix or *Verduras en Escabeche* in the Mexican section of your markets. This is fairly hot with *jalapeño* chiles, or *muy picante* as our Mexican friends say, so adjust to your own taste or substitute milder green chiles. Serve cold as a relish with meats, beans and casseroles.

1 quart

2 medium onions, halved crosswise, cut in wedges
3 large cloves garlic, slivered
4 tablespoons olive or vegetable oil
3 medium carrots, scraped and sliced
¾ cup white vinegar
½ teaspoon salt, or to taste
1 small cauliflower, broken into flowerets
1 can (3½ ounces) plain or
    pickled jalapeño chiles
3 bay leaves
3 medium zucchini, unpeeled, sliced
½ teaspoon oregano
½ teaspoon marjoram
¼ teaspoon ground cumin or ½ teaspoon cumin seed

In large heavy pan, cook onion and garlic slowly in oil until soft, but not brown. Add carrots and stir-fry a couple of minutes. Add vinegar, 1½ cups water and salt. Cover and simmer about 5 minutes. Drop in cauliflowerets and 1 to 2 teaspoons pickling liquid from jalapeños. Simmer gently until nearly tender, about 5 minutes. Add herbs and zucchini, and as many jalapeños as you like—3 or 4 or the entire can. You may cut chiles in strips and remove seeds if you wish. Cover and simmer until zucchini begins to soften, 2 to 5 minutes. Cool, then cover and chill at least overnight. Keep refrigerated.

# Lemon Zucchini Pickles

These are uncooked refrigerator pickles—crunchy and fresh tasting.

2½ pints

6 medium zucchini
1 medium green bell pepper, finely chopped
1 medium onion, finely chopped
1 tablespoon salt
2 teaspoons celery seed
¾ cup sugar
½ cup fresh lemon juice
1 unpeeled lemon, halved, thinly sliced

Cut unpeeled zucchini into thin slices about 1/16th inch thick. Combine in large bowl with green pepper, onion, salt, and celery seed. Mix gently and let stand 1 hour. Dissolve sugar in lemon juice and pour over vegetables. Add lemon slices and mix well. Cover and refrigerate 24 hours. These pickles will keep 3 weeks when stored, uncovered in refrigerator.

# Carrot Dills

Made like cucumber dills, *Carrot Dills* are deliciously different and are pretty pickles for your relish bowl.

4 pints

3 pounds young carrots
Salt
4 teaspoons dill seeds or 8 sprays fresh dill
2 teaspoon mustard seeds
2 cloves garlic
3 cups water
3 cups cider vinegar
¼ teaspoon crushed red pepper
6 tablespoons kosher salt

Scrape carrots and cut into 4-inch sticks (or to fit into pint glass jars). Heat carrots to boiling in 1-inch boiling salted water. Boil 3 or 4 minutes. Drain and pack lengthwise in 4 hot sterilized pint jars. In each jar, put 1 teaspoon dill seed or 2 dill sprays, ½ teaspoon mustard seed, ½ clove garlic, slivered. Combine water, vinegar, red pepper, and salt and heat to boiling. Lower heat and simmer 5 minutes. Pour over carrots, leaving ½ inch head space. Seal at once. Process in *Hot Water Bath* for 5 minutes. Store at least 1 week to develop flavors before serving. Serve chilled.

*Hot Water Bath:* Place jars, not touching each other or kettle on rack in large kettle. Cover jars with boiling water 1-inch above top. Cover kettle, and when water boils again. process the required time. Remove jars from water bath, cool, and store in a cool dark place.

# Refrigerator Carrot Pickles

4 cups small young carrots                                    3 to 4 cups
Salt
3 cups cider vinegar
1 cup water
1½ cups sugar
3 tablespoons mixed pickling spices

Scrape carrots and leave whole or quarter or halve into 4-inch sticks if they are thicker than ½ inch. Cook in boiling salted water about 10 minutes. Drain. In large heavy saucepan combine vinegar, water, sugar and spices. Boil 5 minutes. Add carrots and heat to boiling again. Lower heat and simmer 2 or 3 minutes. Pour into jars or refrigerator dish. Cover, cool, and refrigerate several days before serving. Serve chilled.

# Curry Zucchini Pickles

Curry gives a zippy flavor to these pickles that's different from the usual pickle.

8 pints

5 pounds medium zucchini
1 quart white vinegar
2 cups sugar
¼ cup coarse salt (pickling salt or kosher salt)
¼ cup mustard seed
1 tablespoon celery seed
2 to 3 teaspoons curry powder

Wash zucchini, cut off tips but do not peel. Slice into uniform chunks about ½ inch thick. Combine remaining ingredients in large heavy kettle and heat to boiling. Add zucchini chunks, heat to boiling again, reduce heat, and simmer gently for 10 minutes, stirring frequently. Pour, boiling hot, into sterilized jars filling to ½ inch from top. Seal immediately and process in *Hot Water Bath* (p. 125) 5 minutes.

126

# Zucchini Applesauce

This is good with meats and a great idea when the best apples are expensive and zucchini is abundant and cheap.

1 to 1½ cups

2 medium zucchini
2 apples
½ cup water
½ teaspoon salt
2 whole cloves
2 thin slices unpeeled lemon
6 tablespoons sugar
½ teaspoon cinnamon
1 tablespoon lemon juice

Peel zucchini, halve lengthwise, and slice. Peel and core apples, cut in eighths. Combine in saucepan with water, salt, cloves and lemon slices. Heat to boiling. Cover and cook gently until tender, 25 to 30 minutes. Stir frequently. Uncover and cook rapidly last few minutes if liquid has not cooked down. Remove cloves and lemon. Pour mixture into blender container and whirl until smooth. Blend in sugar, cinnamon and lemon juice. Cover and refrigerate.

# Zucchini Mint Relish

A zippy fresh relish of onions, fresh mint and shredded raw zucchini. Unusual and delicious with grilled or roast lamb or as a side dish with curry.

1½ cups

*1 bunch fresh mint leaves (½ cup when chopped)*
*½ cup finely chopped, sweet white onion*
*1 cup shredded, unpeeled young zucchini*
*Salt*
*1 to 2 tablespoons vinegar*
*Pinch of sugar*

Thoroughly wash a bunch of fresh mint and pull leaves from stems. Wash leaves again and dry on paper towels. Chop finely and pack into a measure. Finely chop an equal amount of sweet white onion. Tip and shred enough tender young zucchini to measure an amount equal to the mint and onion—½ cup each mint and onion, 1 cup shredded zucchini. Salt to taste—zucchini takes plenty— and add 1 to 2 tablespoons vinegar and a pinch of sugar. Cover and chill for several hours before serving.

# Carrot Pepper Relish

4 pints

*6 cups coarsely ground carrots*
*(about 6 to 8 large)*
*2 cups coarsely ground green cabbage*
*2 cups coarsely ground green peppers*
*3 cups coarsely ground onion*
*1 can (4 ounces) green chiles, chopped*

*2 cups brown sugar*
*4 cups cider vinegar*
*3 tablespoons salt (non-iodized)*
*or coarse salt*
*1½ tablespoons dry mustard*
*1 tablespoon celery seed*

Grind vegetables using coarse blade of food chopper or food processor. Combine with chiles and mix well. In large kettle, combine remaining ingredients, mix well and stir in vegetables. Heat to boiling and cook 15 minutes. Stir frequently to prevent sticking and scorching. Pour into sterilized jars, making sure liquid covers vegetables, and seal.

128

# 6

# *Breads and Spreads*

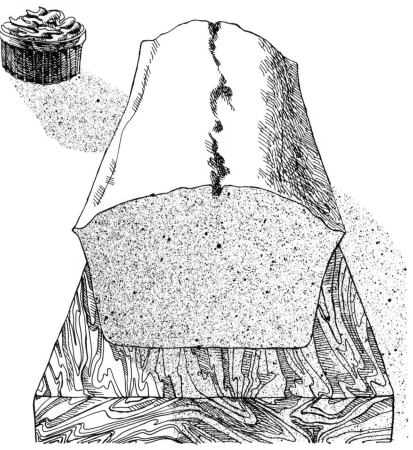

# Zucchini Cheddar Rolls

Sautéed zucchini, herbs and cheese make an unusual filling for these fragrant yeast rolls.

16 to 20 rolls

1 package hot roll mix (or your own recipe for yeast dough rolls)
2 cups shredded zucchini (about 4 medium)
Salt
½ cup chopped onion
4 tablespoons butter or margarine, divided
2 tablespoons minced parsley
½ teaspoon each marjoram and dried dill
1½ cups grated cheddar cheese

Make up hot roll mix by package directions and let rise until doubled in bulk. Shred zucchini onto a sheet of foil and spread it out evenly. Sprinkle lightly with salt and let stand about 20 minutes. Cook onion in 2 tablespoons of the butter until soft. Squeeze excess moisture from zucchini, blot dry with paper towels, and add to onions. Stir over low heat until well coated with butter and lightly cooked, 2 to 3 minutes. Add parsley, marjoram and dill. Soften 2 tablespoons butter and work in cheese to form a smooth paste. Punch raised dough down with your fists and cut into two pieces. Roll each into a rectangle about 8 by 12 inches. Spread with cheese paste, then cover with the zucchini. Roll up and pinch dough along sides to seal in filling. Cut into 8 to 10 equal slices and place cut side down in greased muffin tins. Set in warm place and let rise until doubled, about 30 minutes. Bake at 375°F. 15 to 20 minutes.

# Green Garden Pizza

We seldom think of pizza as bread, though the base for all of these popular out-of-hand feasts is a sturdy yeast dough. Make the typical Italian dough by the recipe that follows, use half a package of hot roll mix for each pizza, or use frozen bread dough.

1 (12-inch) Pizza

½ recipe for Pizza Bread Dough (recipe follows) or
   ½ package hot roll mix (use the rest in rolls or make
   2 pizzas)
½ cup sliced green onions
½ of a green bell pepper, cut into thin strips
3 tablespoons olive oil
2 cups thinly sliced zucchini (2 to 3 medium)
Salt and freshly ground black pepper
½ cup canned tomato sauce (½ of an 8-ounce can)
Oregano
Sweet basil
4 ounces mozzarella cheese, shredded
½ cup freshly grated Parmesan cheese

Prepare dough ahead and have ready to roll when you have filling ingredients assembled. (Follow package directions for hot roll mix.) Cook onion and green pepper in 2 tablespoons oil until soft but not brown, about 2 minutes. Add zucchini, stir until well coated and shiny. Season lightly with salt and pepper. Cover and cook slowly, stirring frequently, until crisp-tender, about 5 minutes. Roll or stretch pizza dough and fit into a 12-inch pizza pan or shape on cookie sheet into a 12-inch circle with a half-inch rim. Brush with 1 tablespoon oil and spread with half the tomato sauce. Crumble a good pinch each of oregano and basil over sauce and spread vegetables in an even layer over that. Cover with rest of sauce and again sprinkle lightly with a little oregano and basil. Top evenly with mozzarella and grated Parmesan. Bake at 425°F. until crust is browned and cheese has melted, about 20 minutes. Cut in wedges and serve warm.

# Pizza Bread Dough

Dough for 2 pizzas

*1 package active dry or cake compressed yeast*
*1¼ cups warm water*
*3½ cups all-purpose flour*
*1 teaspoon salt*
*Dash of pepper*
*2 tablespoons olive oil*
*Cornmeal*

Sprinkle or crumble yeast into ¼ cup warm water. Let stand a minute or two, then stir until it is dissolved. Sift flour, salt and pepper into a large bowl. Make a well in the center and pour in 1 cup warm water, olive oil and the yeast mixture. Mix with wooden spoon or your fingers until you can gather dough into a rough ball. Turn it onto a floured board and knead until smooth and springy, working in a little more flour if needed. Place in an oiled bowl, cover with foil or a towel, and let rise in a warm place until doubled in bulk, 1½ to 2 hours. When ready to make pizzas, punch dough down with your fists and divide into two balls. Knead each lightly, as needed, to work out air bubbles. Stretch and flatten to desired size and place in pizza pans or on cookie sheet lightly sprinkled with corn meal.

### VARIATIONS

**Italian Sausage Pizza:** Remove casings from ½ pound fresh sweet or hot Italian sausages. Cook sausage until browned and crumbly. Drain and sprinkle over top layer of sauce in Green Garden Pizza (above). Top with cheese and bake.

**Anchovy Pizza:** Drain and chop a can of anchovies. Sprinkle over top layer of sauce in Green Garden Pizza (above). Top with cheese and bake. Canned kipper snacks, chopped, are great here too.

# Zucchini Carrot Wheat Bread

There are carrot breads and zucchini breads, for which there are several recipes in this book. Each vegetable adds moisture and its own unique flavor. I've worked out this recipe with both of them plus the extra nutty goodness of whole wheat flour. Texture is better if breads are baked in small loaf pans and allowed to mellow several days before you cut them.

2 loaves

1 cup finely shredded raw carrots
1½ cups shredded, unpeeled zucchini
   (more mature zucchini may be used)
½ cup chopped pitted dates
½ cup seedless raisins
1 cup whole wheat flour
1½ cups all-purpose flour
2 teaspoons baking powder
½ teaspoon soda

1 teaspoon cinnamon
½ teaspoon nutmeg
½ teaspoon ground cloves
¾ teaspoon salt
3 eggs
1¼ cups sugar
¾ cup vegetable oil
¼ cup honey
1 cup thinly sliced,
   natural skin almonds

Shred carrots. Shred zucchini into a strainer and allow moisture to drain briefly while you prepare rest of ingredients. With wet kitchen scissors, cut dates into pieces. Rinse raisins in hot water and blot dry on paper towels. Mix fruits on sheet of foil with 2 tablespoons of the flour. Sift together or thoroughly mix the flours, baking powder, soda, spices and salt. Beat eggs at high speed on electric mixer until very light. Gradually beat in sugar, beating to keep mixture light. Slowly beat in oil until thoroughly blended and mixture is light. With rubber scraper, blend in flour mixture and stir until smooth but do not beat. Blend in carrots, zucchini, honey, floured fruits and nuts. Stir until well mixed. Turn batter into 2 greased, small loaf pans (8½ x 4½ x 2½), bake at 350°F. 1 hour to 1 hour and 15 minutes. Tester should come out clean when stuck in center of bread. Cool in pans 10 minutes. Remove to wire racks to cool. Foil wrap and store overnight before slicing.

SEE ALSO *Zucchini Walnut Bread* (p. 173)

# Carrot Raisin Bread

A colorful yeast bread given the extra flavor boost of grated raw carrots, raisins, and orange zest.

2 loaves

*1½ cups grated raw carrots (about 2 medium)*
*1 cup milk*
*3 tablespoons butter or margarine*
*2 packages active dry yeast or 2 cakes compressed yeast*
*1 cup warm water*
*2 tablespoons sugar*
*2 teaspoons salt*
*2 tablespoons honey*
*2 tablespoons coarsely grated orange peel*
*½ teaspoon nutmeg*
*Generous pinch of ground cloves*
*1 egg, beaten*
*6 to 6½ cups unbleached all-purpose flour*
*1 cup seedless raisins*

Grate carrots and set aside. Heat milk and butter in small saucepan over low heat just until butter is melted. Sprinkle yeast over warm water in a large warm mixing bowl. Stir until it's dissolved. Blend in sugar, salt, honey, orange peel, spices, egg and warmed milk. With wooden spoon, beat in 3 cups of the flour then beat in carrots and raisins. Blend in 3 more cups of flour until dough is smooth. Turn out onto a board sprinkled with part of the remaining ½ cup flour. Knead, adding flour as necessary until dough is smooth, springy, and no longer sticky. Grease a large bowl with oil, put dough in it, and turn to coat evenly. Cover with foil, then a folded towel. Place in a warm spot and let rise until doubled in bulk, about 1 hour. Slap raised dough on board to remove any air bubbles and shape into a smooth loaf. Place in 2 greased loaf pans (8½ x 4½ x 2½ inches). Bake at 400°F. about 30 minutes, until richly browned and bread sounds hollow when rapped with your knuckles. Turn out of pan onto wire rack to cool. Great for spreads, sandwiches or toast.

135

# Carrot Date Nut Bread

Called bread, this is as moistly rich and delicious as a cake, only not as sweet. A good idea for holiday gifts.

2 loaves

1½ cups sliced, scraped carrots (about 5 or 6)
1 seedless orange, cut in pieces
¾ cup buttermilk
3 cups all-purpose flour
2 teaspoons soda
1 teaspoon baking powder
1 teaspoon cinnamon
½ teaspoon nutmeg
1 teaspoon salt
2 large eggs
1¼ cups sugar
¾ cup light vegetable oil
1 cup slivered, pitted dates
1 cup coarsely chopped walnuts

Put carrots in heavy saucepan with 1 cup water and ½ teaspoon each salt and sugar. Cover and simmer until tender, 25 to 30 minutes. Drain, if all moisture has not evaporated. Put orange, buttermilk and carrots in blender. Whirl until puréed. You should have about 2 cups of purée. Sift flour with dry ingredients except sugar. In mixing bowl, beat eggs and beat in sugar, oil and carrot purée. Stir in dry mixture and mix until well blended but do not beat. Stir in dates and nuts. Spread in 2 greased and floured small loaf pans (about 8½ x 4½ x 2½ inches). Bake at 350°F. 45 minutes to 1 hour, or until pick inserted near center comes out clean. Remove from pans to wire racks. Cool overnight before cutting.

# Carrot Wheat Muffins

Moist wheaty muffins enriched with carrots and molasses. Nice for luncheon or supper with soup or salad.

12 muffins

1 cup whole wheat flour
1 cup all-purpose flour
3 teaspoons baking powder
¾ teaspoon salt
¼ cup sugar
1 cup coarsely grated carrots
  (2 medium or 1 large)

1 teaspoon grated fresh
  orange peel
1 egg
1 cup milk
¼ cup molasses
¼ cup vegetable oil

Spoon each flour into measuring cup. Level off and sift with baking powder, salt and sugar into mixing bowl. Stir in carrots and orange peel. In small bowl, beat egg with milk, molasses and oil. Stir into dry mixture just enough to moisten well but do not beat. Fill greased muffin pans ¾ full. Bake at 400°F. about 25 minutes. Serve warm with butter.

# Carrot Marmalade

An interesting and unusual recipe. This was a winner in the Holtville, California Carrot Carnival. It has a lemony tang and reminds me of the English bitter orange marmalade.

2 ½-pints

2 cups coarsely grated carrots
  (about 1 pound)
Grated peel of 1 large orange
½ cup fresh orange juice

Grated peel of 1 large lemon
⅓ cup fresh lemon juice
2 cups sugar
1 cup water

Mix all ingredients together in heavy saucepan. Heat to boiling and simmer gently until thickened to desired consistency, about 20 minutes. Stir frequently to prevent sticking and scorching. Pour into sterilized glasses and seal.

137

# Carrot Peanut Butter Spread

This crunchy new way with an old favorite seems to lighten peanut butter and give a fresh garden flavor to it.

¾ cup

¾ cup grated or finely shredded raw carrots
½ cup chunky-grind peanut butter
1½ tablespoons mayonnaise
1 tablespoon honey, or to taste
1 teaspoon grated fresh orange peel

Combine all ingredients and stir until well mixed. Spread on bread, toast or crackers.

# Carrot Walnut Spread

1½ cups

1 cup shredded raw carrot
½ cup finely chopped walnuts
2 tablespoons pickle relish
3 tablespoons mayonnaise
Salt
Lemon juice
Raisin or whole wheat bread

Combine carrots with walnuts, pickle relish, mayonnaise and salt and lemon juice to taste. Spread on raisin or wheat bread.

# Crunchy Egg Salad Filling

1 pint

4 hard-cooked eggs
¾ cup grated raw carrots
¼ cup chopped celery
2 strips crisp-cooked bacon, crumbled
2 teaspoons lemon juice
1 teaspoon mild prepared mustard
1 teaspoon grated onion
Salt and pepper
Mayonnaise

Chop eggs and mix with carrots, celery, bacon, lemon juice, mustard, and grated onion. Add salt and pepper to taste and enough mayonnaise to make the filling of proper spreading consistency.

# Date Carrot Spread

An instant spread for morning toast, lunch sandwich or afternoon tea break.

1 cup

1 cup scraped, diced carrots (2 or 3)
1 cup coarsely chopped, pitted dates
2 tablespoons orange juice
1 teaspoon grated orange peel
Buttered toast or dark nut bread
Cream cheese
Mayonnaise and pickle relish

Grind together or finely chop in blender or food processor the diced carrots and chopped dates. Add orange juice and orange peel. Mix well. Cover and store in refrigerator. Spread on buttered toast or thinly sliced dark nut bread, with cream cheese, if you like. Vary for sandwiches with a little mayonnaise and pickle relish.

139

# Zucchini Egg Sandwich

One serving

A meal-in-hand in a hurry, this sandwich has a different, gardeny flavor.

For each sandwich, dice enough young, unpeeled zucchini to make ½ cup. Finely chop 1 green onion. Stir-fry together in a small skillet in about 2 teaspoons margarine or oil until soft, a couple of minutes. Beat 1 egg lightly with 1 tablespoon sour cream and salt and pepper to taste. Pour over vegetables and stir lightly with fork, then let egg brown lightly on bottom. Turn and brown second side lightly. Serve between slices of crisp hot toast.

# Bean Sprout Sandwich

One serving

Saute chopped zucchini and green onion as described above in *Zucchini Egg Sandwich.* Top with a handful of fresh bean sprouts—or lentil sprouts if you prefer. Beat 2 eggs lightly and season with salt and pepper and a teaspoon of soy sauce. Pour over vegetables and cook until lightly set and browned on each side. Serve with crisp hot toast.

# 7

# Cakes, Pies, Puddings, and Cookies

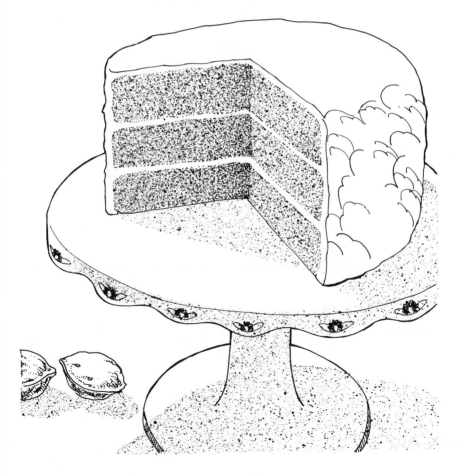

# Cherry Zucchini Cakes

Moist and fruity, these are rich yet delicate. A great cake for the holidays and much easier than fruitcake. Be sure to use the thinly sliced natural almonds as specified.

2 loaf cakes

2 cups finely shredded (or grated) unpeeled zucchini
1 cup candied cherries, coarsely chopped
2 cups all-purpose flour plus 2 tablespoons extra
½ teaspoon baking powder
2 teaspoons soda
½ teaspoon salt
1 teaspoon cinnamon
1 teaspoon nutmeg
½ teaspoon allspice
3 eggs
2 cups sugar
¾ cup light salad oil
2 teaspoons vanilla
¼ teaspoon almond extract
1½ cups thinly sliced natural skin almonds

Grate zucchini. Mix cherries and extra flour. Sift together flour, baking powder, soda, salt and spices. Beat eggs on electric mixer until very light and fluffy. Gradually beat in sugar and oil. With rubber scraper or on very low speed of mixer, blend in dry mixture, vanilla and almond extract, zucchini, cherries and almonds. Turn into two greased and floured small loaf pans. (8½ x 4½ x 2½ inches). Bake 50 minutes to 1 hour at 350°F. until sides shrink slightly and tops spring back when lightly touched. Cool cakes in pan about 10 minutes, then turn out onto wire racks to cool. Sift powdered sugar over cakes before cutting, if you wish, or drizzle with *Orange Glaze* or *Lemon Glaze* (see index).

# Zucchini Chocolate Cake

This cake is moist and rich with zucchini and buttermilk and has a light chocolate flavor sparked with orange. Sometimes I make it with shredded, raw zucchini and at other times with puréed cooked zucchini. The texture seems a little finer and more moist with the purée, but the difference is slight. As with all the zucchini and carrot cakes, this one looks showy baked in a bundt pan, but the texture is finer and lighter when baked in a sheet pan, in layers, or in small loaves.

Large sheet cake or 2 layers

2 cups sliced, unpeeled zucchini (2 or 3 medium)
    (see note about shredded zucchini)
Salt
2 cups all-purpose flour
1 teaspoon soda
1 teaspoon baking powder
1 teaspoon cinnamon
½ teaspoon nutmeg
¼ cup unsweetened cocoa
3 large eggs
2 cups sugar
½ cup vegetable oil
¾ cup buttermilk
1 teaspoon vanilla
1 teaspoon grated fresh orange peel
1 cup coarsely chopped pecans or walnuts
Orange Glaze

Put zucchini in saucepan with ½ cup water (or orange juice, if you like) and ½ teaspoon salt. Cover and cook gently until tender enough to mash or purée, about 10 minutes. Drain if necessary and mash or purée in blender until smooth. You should have 1 cup purée. Sift flour with soda, baking powder, spices, cocoa, and ¼ teaspoon salt. Beat eggs in large bowl of mixer until very light. Gradually beat in sugar until mixture is fluffy and a pale ivory color. Slowly beat in oil, beating to keep mixture light. Combine zucchini purée and buttermilk. Stir flour mixture into eggs alternately with buttermilk mix. Blend on low speed of mixer or with rubber scraper until well mixed. Stir in vanilla, orange peel and nuts. Pour into greased and floured sheet-cake pan (13 x 9 x 2 inches) or two round (9 inch) layer-cake pans. Bake at 350°F. 40 to 50 minutes, until cake shrinks slightly from sides and tester is clean when stuck in center and removed. Cool layers 10 minutes, remove to wire racks to cool completely. Frost with *Cream Cheese Frosting* (see index) or a favorite chocolate icing. Cool sheet cake in pan on wire rack about 10 minutes. Drizzle with *Orange Glaze* and cool completely.

### VARIATION

**Shredded Zucchini Chocolate Cake:** Use 2 cups shredded raw, unpeeled zucchini in place of cooked zucchini puree in preceding recipe. Add to egg mixture along with buttermilk and dry ingredients.

## Orange Glaze

Stir into 1 cup powdered sugar, sifted: 1 tablespoon orange juice, 1 teaspoon shredded fresh orange peel, and 1 tablespoon bubbling hot, melted butter or margarine. Blend until smooth.

# Zucchini Granola Torte

A moist and chewy meringue-type torte enlivened with green flecks of zucchini and crunchy granola bits. May be served as a dessert with whipped cream or cut into strips as cookies.

9-inch torte or 3½ dozen cookies

1 cup finely diced, unpeeled zucchini
1 tablespoon fresh lemon juice
1 cup lightly crushed packaged granola
½ cup chopped walnuts or pecans
¾ cup all-purpose flour
1½ teaspoons baking powder
¼ teaspoon salt
1 teaspoon cinnamon
2 large eggs
¾ cup sugar
1 teaspoon vanilla

Combine zucchini and lemon juice, mixing well. Lightly crush granola—but don't smash it into crumbs—and chop nuts. Sift flour with baking powder, salt and cinnamon. Beat eggs until very light and beat in sugar until mixture is fluffy and a pale cream color. With rubber scraper, stir in flour until batter is smooth. Blend in zucchini, granola, nuts and vanilla. Spread in a greased and floured 9-inch square pan (or spread thinner in an oblong pan 13 x 9 x 2 inches for cookies). Bake torte at 325°F. 30 to 40 minutes, until top is puffed and crusty looking. Bake cookies 25 to 30 minutes. Cool in pan. Cut torte in squares or oblongs and serve with whipped cream or fruit compote, if you like. Cut cookies into strips.

SEE ALSO *Zucchini Nut Cake* (p. 175)

146

# Casa Bateman Carrot Cake

I made this cake for my last book, *Fifty Great Buffet Parties* published by Doubleday (© 1974). It is still a favorite at our house and too good to leave out of this collection. I've since revised the mixing method and reduced the amount of vegetable oil. It makes a lighter cake, still moist and rich, and simply yummy.

2 layers or 1 large sheet cake

*3 cups finely shredded raw carrots*
*2 cups unbleached white flour*
*2 teaspoons soda*
*2 teaspoons cinnamon*
*1 teaspoon nutmeg*
*¼ teaspoon salt*
*4 eggs*
*2 cups sugar*
*1 cup light vegetable oil*
*1 teaspoon vanilla*
*1 teaspoon grated fresh lemon or orange peel*
*1 cup coarsely chopped pecans or walnuts*

Grate carrots with medium side of grater. Sift together flour, soda, spices and salt. Beat eggs until very light, then gradually beat in sugar until mixture is fluffy and a pale cream color. Slowly add oil, beating to keep mixture light. With rubber scraper, blend in flour mixture, then carrots, vanilla, peel and nuts. Spread in greased and floured sheet-cake pan (13 x 9 x 2 inches) or two round layer-cake pans. Bake at 350°F., 45 minutes to 1 hour for the large cake, 35 to 40 minutes for the layers, or until tester is clean when stuck in center and removed. Cool layers in pan 10 minutes, then remove to wire racks to cool. Frost with *Cream Cheese Frosting* or *Tropical Butter Frosting* (see index). Cool sheet cake in pan on wire rack 10 minutes then glaze with *Orange Glaze* or *Lemon Glaze* (see index). Cool and cut into squares.

# Tropical Carrot Cake

There are numerous carrot cake recipes around and all are moistly delicious, pack well, keep well, and are easy to make. This one is a little different with pineapple and coconut inside and in the luscious frosting. It's my favorite.

3 layers or large sheet cake

2 cups all-purpose flour
2 teaspoons baking powder
1 teaspoon soda
½ teaspoon salt
1 teaspoon cinnamon
½ teaspoon nutmeg
½ teaspoon allspice
2 cups grated raw carrots
1 can (8-½ ounces) crushed pineapple, lightly drained
1 cup chopped walnuts
4 eggs
2 cups sugar
1¼ cups light salad oil
½ cup flaked coconut
Tropical Butter Frosting

Sift together all dry ingredients except sugar. Prepare carrots, pineapple and nuts. Grease and flour 3 (9-inch) round cake pans or an oblong pan (13 x 9 x 2 inches). Beat eggs lightly and beat in sugar. Stir in oil, dry mixture, carrots and pineapple (you should have ¾ cup pineapple). Mix well. Stir in walnuts and coconut. Spread evenly in pans. Bake at 350°F. 35 to 40 minutes for layers; 45 to 60 minutes for large cake, or until sides shrink slightly and top springs back when touched. Cool layers in pans 10 minutes then turn out on wire racks to cool completely. Stack and frost with *Tropical Butter Frosting* or *Cream Cheese Frosting* (see index). Decorate top with shredded orange peel. Frost sheet in pan or simply sprinkle with powdered sugar.

# Tropical Butter Frosting

¼ cup butter or margarine
1 pound powdered sugar, sifted
¼ cup lightly drained, canned crushed pineapple
2 tablespoons sour cream
1 teaspoon vanilla
¼ teaspoon salt
2 teaspoons coarsely grated fresh orange peel
¾ cup flaked coconut, chopped

Beat butter until soft and gradually beat in sugar, pineapple and sour cream alternately until frosting is fluffy and smooth. Blend in vanilla, salt, orange peel and coconut.

# Cream Cheese Frosting

The favorite gilding for carrot cakes.

2 packages (3 ounces each) cream cheese
1 package (1 pound) powdered sugar, sifted
2 tablespoons orange or lemon juice
1 teaspoon vanilla
1 teaspoon grated fresh lemon or orange peel

In small bowl of mixer beat cream cheese until soft and light. Gradually beat in powdered sugar. Thin as you beat to a good spreading consistency with orange or lemon juice. Flavor with vanilla and lemon or orange peel. Enough to fill and frost 2- or 3-layer cake.

# 24 Carat Cake

The carats are the golden carrots used in this luscious spicy cake—one of the prize winners in the annual Carrot Carnival held in the past in Holtville, California's "Carrot Capital of the World."

2 layers or 1 sheet cake

*¾ cup sieved cooked carrots (about 6 medium)*
*Pinch each of salt and sugar*
*2 cups sifted all-purpose flour*
*2 teaspoons baking powder*
*½ teaspoon soda*
*¼ teaspoon salt*
*1 teaspoon cinnamon*
*½ teaspoon mace*
*½ teaspoon ground cloves*
*Dash of ground ginger*
*1 cup butter or margarine*
*1 cup sugar*
*1 cup brown sugar*
*4 eggs, separated*
*1 cup chopped walnuts*
*Golden Carrot Frosting*

Scrape and slice carrots. Cook covered in 1 inch of boiling water with a pinch of each salt and sugar until tender, about 25 minutes. Drain, saving ¼ cup of the cooking liquid. Press through sieve or purée in blender. Sift together all dry ingredients except sugar. Cream butter and sugars together until light and fluffy. Beat in egg yolks, one at a time. Blend in dry ingredients, ⅓ at a time alternately with carrot purée and liquid. Stir in nuts. Beat egg whites until stiff and gently fold into batter. Spread in two greased and floured 9-inch round cake pans or a sheet pan, 9 x 13 x 2 inches. Bake at 350°F. 40 to 45 minutes, a little longer for large cake, or until top springs back when lightly touched. Cool layers a few minutes and turn out onto wire racks to cool. Frost with *Golden Carrot Frosting*. Frost sheet cake in pan.

## Golden Carrot Frosting

¼ *cup butter or margarine*
3 *cups powdered sugar, sifted*
¼ *cup sieved, cooked carrot*
2 *tablespoons orange juice*
1½ *teaspoons grated fresh orange peel*
*Dash of salt*

Beat butter or margarine until soft and gradually beat in powdered sugar alternately with cooked carrot and orange juice. When smooth and fluffy, stir in grated fresh orange peel and a dash of salt.

# Old-Fashioned Carrot Cake

This spicy moist cake can be stirred together in a few minutes. It has no eggs and very little shortening, yet it tastes rich.

1 large sheet cake

1 cup grated raw carrots (about 2 medium)
1 cup seedless raisins or ½ cup each of raisins and
   coarsely cut dates
1½ cups sugar
1 teaspoon cinnamon
1 teaspoon nutmeg
½ teaspoon ground cloves
1½ cups water
3 tablespoons vegetable shortening
1 cup chopped walnuts
2 cups all-purpose flour (unbleached preferred)
2 teaspoons soda
¼ teaspoon salt

Combine carrots, raisins, sugar, spices, water, and shortening. Boil 5 minutes and pour into mixing bowl. Let stand until completely cool (2 or 3 hours). Prepare walnuts and sift measured flour with soda and salt. Combine and stir into carrot mixture. Spread in greased and floured oblong pan (8 x 12 or 9 x 13 inches). Bake at 325°F. until top springs back when touched lightly, about 1 hour for larger pan, 1 hour and 15 minutes for smaller, thicker cake. Cool, cut into squares, and serve from pan.

SEE ALSO *Almond Carrot Cake* (p. 177)
   *Great Grandma's Sheep-Wagon Carrot Cake* (p. 178)

# Quick-Mix Carrot Cake

This quick-mix carrot cake is not as rich and moist as the "scratch" carrot cakes but is plenty rich, flavorful, and very easy to make.

1 sheet cake

1 package (2-layer size) yellow or spice cake mix
1 teaspoon cinnamon ⎫
1 teaspoon nutmeg ⎬      For yellow cake mix only,
½ teaspoon allspice ⎭
⅓ cup sour cream
1 cup grated raw carrots
½ cup seedless raisins
¾ cup chopped walnuts or pecans
1 teaspoon grated fresh lemon or orange peel
Powdered sugar or
Favorite Butter or Cream Cheese Frosting (see index)

To the dry yellow cake mix, add cinnamon, nutmeg and allspice. Mix well. Prepare either cake mix by package directions replacing ¼ cup of liquid with ⅓ cup sour cream. Blend into mixed batter the grated carrots, raisins, nuts, and lemon or orange peel. Spread batter evenly in a greased and floured sheet cake pan (13 x 9 x 2 inches). Bake at 350° 40 minutes to 1 hour, or until pick inserted in center comes out clean. Cool in pan. Sprinkle with powdered sugar or spread with your favorite frosting.

# Carrot Almond Torte

This is not a fluffy, dry cake, but a moist tender torte, light and spongy, with plenty of eggs. No fat is used. Ground sweet almonds and puréed carrots contribute to its unusual flavor and delicacy.

1 spring-form torte or 2 layers

2 cups sliced, scraped carrots
  (3 to 4 medium)
Salt
Sugar
6 ounces blanched, dry almonds
½ cup all-purpose flour
1 teaspoon baking powder

2 tablespoons Grand Marnier
  (or other orange liqueur)
6 eggs, separated
1½ cups sugar
1 teaspoon grated fresh orange peel
1 cup whipping cream

Put carrots in saucepan with 1 cup water and ½ teaspoon each salt and sugar. Cover tightly and cook until very tender, about 25 minutes. Meanwhile, whirl almonds, one half at a time, in blender until ground to a texture about like coarse corn meal. Mix with flour, baking powder, and a pinch of salt. Drain carrots if necessary. Whirl in blender with 1 tablespoon Grand Marnier to make 1 cup smooth purée. Grease a 9-inch spring-form pan or 2 round (9-inch) layer-cake pans. Preheat oven to 325°F. Beat egg yolks until very light and gradually beat in sugar until mixture is fluffy and a pale ivory color. With rubber scraper, lightly but thoroughly blend in carrots, orange peel and almond mixture. With soapy suds, wash beaters, rinse, and wipe dry of every bit of egg yolk. Beat whites until peaks are sharp and upright when beaters are withdrawn. Gently fold a big spoonful of whites into batter to lighten it. Then fold in the rest, lightly and quickly to retain the air already beaten into mixture. Turn into greased pan. Bake at 325°F. about 50 minutes to 1 hour for the spring form, 35 to 40 minutes for layers. Cool torte completely in pans set on wire racks. Gently remove from pans. Put layers together with softly whipped cream flavored with 1 tablespoon Grand Marnier. Top with cream. Cut taller torte into wedges and serve with the flavored cream.

# Shaggy Carrot Cookies

Shredded raw carrot gives these rich oatmeal cookies a subtle new flavor and texture.

8 to 10 dozen cookies

1 cup finely shredded raw carrots (2 to 3 medium)
2 cups unbleached white flour
½ teaspoon soda
½ teaspoon baking powder
Dash of salt
1 cup shortening (part butter or
    margarine for flavor)
1 cup granulated sugar
1 cup brown sugar
2 eggs
1 teaspoon vanilla
2 cups uncooked oats
1 cup flaked or shredded coconut
1½ cups chopped walnuts

Scrape and shred carrots; set aside. Sift together flour, soda, baking powder and salt. In electric mixer, beat shortening and gradually beat in sugars until mixture is creamy and light. Beat in eggs, one at a time. On low speed or with rubber scraper, gradually blend in the rest of the ingredients. Drop by teaspoonful onto greased cookie sheets. Bake at 350°F. 18 to 22 minutes, or until lightly browned. Remove to wire racks to cool. Store in tightly covered container.

## VARIATIONS

**Holiday Shaggies:** Add ½ cup of chopped candied fruits to the dough. Press strip of candied cherry into each cookie before baking.

155

# Carrot Orange Cookies

This easy cookie has a hint of orange and nutmeg that is nice with the grated carrot. Gratefully, these are not too sweet.

5 to 6 dozen cookies

1 cup grated raw carrots
  (2 medium small or 1 large)
1¼ cups all-purpose flour
1 teaspoon baking powder
Pinch of salt
½ teaspoon nutmeg
½ cup butter or margarine
½ cup sugar
1 egg
1½ teaspoons grated fresh orange peel
1 tablespoon orange juice
¾ cup chopped walnuts or pecans

Grate carrots and sift flour with baking powder, salt and nutmeg. Cream butter with sugar until fluffy and beat in egg, orange peel and juice. Stir in flour mixture alternately with carrots until dough is well mixed. Blend in nuts. Drop by overloaded teaspoon onto greased cookie sheets. Bake at 375°F. 15 to 20 minutes, until lightly tanned. Remove to wire racks to cool. Store in tightly covered container.

# Almond Carrot Macaroons

Grated carrots and ground almonds combine beautifully in these chewy, moist macaroons. An unusual recipe.

3 dozen cookies

2 cups ground, blanched almonds
1 cup grated raw carrots (about 2 medium)
2 egg whites
Pinch of salt
1 cup sugar
½ teaspoon vanilla
¼ teaspoon almond extract

To grind almonds, put into blender (or food processor) about ½ cup at a time, and whirl until ground into an almond meal. Grate carrots. Beat egg whites with salt and gradually beat in sugar. When half of it has been added, begin adding almond meal. Beat until all is added. Stir in carrots and flavorings. Drop in small mounds 1½ inches apart on greased and floured cookie sheets. Let macaroons stand overnight. Bake at 300°F. 25 to 30 minutes. Let stand until cold and carefully remove from cookie sheet with small spatula. Store in tightly covered container.

SEE ALSO *Lemon Zucchini Cookies* (p. 174)

# Grated Carrot Pie

Grated raw carrot gives an unusual flavor and crunchy top to this custard pie. It will remind you of a delicious coconut custard.

6 to 7 servings

*Pastry for a 9-inch pie (your own recipe or a mix)*
*1 cup coarsely grated raw carrots (2 to 3 medium)*
*3 tablespoons butter or margarine*
*½ cup sugar*
*2 tablespoons flour*
*3 eggs*
*1½ cups undiluted, evaporated milk*
*Pinch of salt*
*¼ teaspoon cinnamon*
*¼ teaspoon ground cloves*
*¼ teaspoon nutmeg*

Roll pastry and fit into a 9-inch glass pie dish. Turn ½ inch of edge under and press to rim with tines of fork. Grate carrots. Cream butter and sugar together and blend in flour. Beat in eggs one at a time. Stir in milk, seasonings and carrots. Pour into pastry shell and bake at 425°F. 15 minutes. Reduce heat to 350°F. and bake 20 to 30 minutes longer. Custard should still be a trifle quivery in the center. Cool on wire rack.

# Carrot Lemon Pie

A prize winner at the Holtville, California Carrot Carnival, this great favorite is a happy way to get your pie lovers to eat carrots.

6 to 8 servings

1 baked 9-inch pie shell
1 package (3¼ ounces) lemon pudding and pie filling
1 cup sugar, divided
1¼ cups water
2 eggs, separated
1 tablespoon lemon juice
1 cup grated, fresh young carrots (about 2 to 3 medium)

Bake and cool pie shell ahead. Prepare lemon pie filling by directions on package, using ½ cup of the sugar, the water, and 2 egg yolks. Cool. Add lemon juice and ¼ cup sugar to carrots; stir into lemon filling and spread in pie shell. Beat egg whites until foamy, then gradually beat in remaining ¼ cup sugar, beating continually until meringue stands in somewhat stiff peaks but is still glossy. Spread lightly over pie. Bake at 350°F. 10 to 15 minutes, until delicately browned. Cool 2 to 4 hours before cutting.

# Carrot Pecan Pie

This is another prize-winner recipe from the Holtville Carrot Carnival. The pecan topping makes it richer and more festive than the traditional carrot custard pie. It will give your favorite pumpkin pie a run for the money. Try it and see!

8 servings

*Pastry for a 9-inch pie*
*(your own recipe or a mix)*
*2 cups sliced, scraped carrots*
*4 tablespoons butter or margarine*
*½ cup sugar*
*2 eggs*
*1 cup milk (can be evaporated)*
*½ teaspoon nutmeg*

*½ teaspoon cinnamon*
*⅛ teaspoon ground ginger*
*¼ teaspoon salt*

PECAN TOPPING:

*1 tablespoon butter or margarine*
*1 tablespoon brown sugar*
*½ cup pecans, halves or pieces*

Make pastry ahead, line glass pie pan, and chill while you make filling. Cook carrots covered in 1 cup water (with a pinch each of salt and sugar) until very tender, about 30 minutes. Drain, if any liquid remains, and whirl carrots in blender until smooth. You should have 1 cup of purée. Cream butter with ¼ cup sugar. With whisk, beat eggs lightly and whisk in remaining ¼ cup sugar, the carrot purée, milk, spices and salt. Whisk in the creamed butter and sugar until mixture is blended evenly. Pour into pastry and set in oven preheated to 450°F. Bake 15 minutes. Reduce heat to 325°F. Remove pie and spread with Pecan Topping. Bake about 40 minutes longer, or until firm. Cool completely before cutting. Serve in small wedges with softly whipped cream.

**Pecan Topping:** In small saucepan, melt butter and add brown sugar. Stir over low heat until sugar melts, just a few seconds. Add pecans, remove from heat, and stir until pecans are coated with the syrup.

SEE ALSO *Golden Carrot Pie* (p. 179)

# Carrot Pudding Ring

You may serve this spicy carrot ring warm as a pudding with the delightful *Apricot Ginger Sauce* or frost it with the luscious *Cream Cheese Frosting* and call it a cake. It is delicious either way and quickly, easily made. Some cooks serve this as a vegetable, but I think it belongs among the desserts.

6 to 8 servings

¾ cup vegetable shortening
1 cup brown sugar, firmly packed
1¼ cups all-purpose flour
¼ teaspoon soda
1 teaspoon baking powder
Pinch of salt
2 cups grated raw carrots

Grated peel of 1 lemon
2 tablespoons fresh lemon juice
2 eggs
⅓ cup seedless raisins or
    diced mixed candied fruits
½ cup chopped walnuts or pecans
Apricot Ginger Sauce

Cream shortening and sugar together until well blended. Sift flour with soda, baking powder and salt. Prepare grated carrots, lemon peel and juice. Preheat oven to 350°F. and grease a 6-cup ring mold. Add eggs, one at a time, to creamed mixture and beat until light. Blend in carrots, lemon peel and juice. With rubber scraper, blend in flour mixture, raisins and nuts. Spread in greased ring mold. Bake at 350°F. 35 to 40 minutes, until firm on top and tester is clean when stuck into pudding and removed. Let stand in pan a moment, then loosen and carefully turn out onto serving plate or wire rack. Serve warm, as a pudding with *Apricot Ginger Sauce*, cool and frost as desired, or drizzle with the light *Orange Glaze*.

## Apricot Ginger Sauce          2 cups

Whirl in blender until smooth: 1 cup apricot preserves or jam with ¾ cup apricot nectar, 2 tablespoons lemon juice and ¼ cup cream sherry or Madeira wine. Heat to boiling in small saucepan with 2 tablespoons finely chopped, candied ginger. Simmer a few minutes and serve hot with pudding.

161

# Granddaughter's Steamed Pudding

Every grandmother has her favorite steamed pudding for the holidays—and some still make them. Granddaughter is more likely to go for this easier one which starts with a cake mix and contains grated sweet carrots, molasses and raisins for the old-fashioned moist texture and flavor. This pudding is lighter, of course, than the traditional fruit and suet-laden holiday pudding but perfect for our contemporary tastes.

8 servings

*1 cup grated raw carrots (2 or 3 medium)*
*¼ cup seedless raisins*
*¼ cup chopped mixed candied fruits*
*1 package spice-cake mix (2-layer size)*
*but use only half for this recipe*

*1 egg*
*Water*
*¼ cup dark molasses*
*½ cup chopped walnuts or peca*
*Hard Sauce or Lemon Sauce*

🐟 Prepare grated carrots. Rinse raisins in hot water and dry on paper towels. Mix raisins with candied fruits and carrots. Empty cake mix into a bowl or a glass measure and put aside half of it (see note for using the rest of package). Put the half package of mix in the large bowl of electric mixer and beat with egg and half the water specified on the mix label. Blend in molasses, mixed fruits and carrots and nuts. Turn into a well-buttered 1½-quart mold or metal bowl. Fill mold about ⅔ full. Cover with lid or two thicknesses of buttered foil and secure with a rubber band or string. This is very important, as water must not get into the batter. Set mold on rack or trivet in a deep kettle. Pour in hot water halfway up the mold. Cover kettle and steam 2½ hours. Keep water simmering and add more to keep the level the same. Unmold pudding and serve hot, in small wedges, with *Hard Sauce* or warm *Lemon Sauce*.

### NOTES

**To Reheat:** If you make this ahead, cool in mold, covered. Steam 1 hour on trivet in kettle of simmering water, same as before.

**About Cake Mix:** You may make up the whole package of mix and bake half of it as an 8- or 9-inch cake. Use the rest of the batter for the steamed pudding. Or, seal unused half securely for use later.

# Hard Sauce

6 tablespoons butter or margarine
1½ cups powdered sugar, sifted
1 tablespoon hot water
1 teaspoon vanilla
1 to 2 tablespoons (or to taste) Brandy,
    Bourbon, Sherry or dark rum
Nutmeg

Soften butter or margarine and beat in powdered sugar adding hot water as you beat to make the sauce light and fluffy. Flavor as desired with vanilla and Brandy, Bourbon, Sherry, or dark rum, or to taste. I like to add a flick of nutmeg, too.

# Lemon Sauce

2 cups

¾ cup sugar
2 tablespoons cornstarch
Dash of salt
Dash of nutmeg
1¾ cups water
2 tablespoons butter or margarine
3 tablespoons (or more) fresh lemon juice
1 teaspoon grated lemon peel

In saucepan, blend together sugar, cornstarch, dash of salt and nutmeg. Stir in water, butter or margarine and lemon juice. Heat to boiling over medium heat, then stir until sauce is clear and thickened. Add lemon peel and more lemon juice if needed. Flavor should be tart-sweet. Serve warm with pudding.

# 8

# *Good Neighbor Recipe Exchange*

# French Casserole

Mary Jane's friends call this her French casserole. You will realize that it is her easy, oven version of France's garlicky, riotously colorful Ratatouille. It is absolutely wonderful—and so easy.

6 to 8 servings

1 medium eggplant, unpeeled, cut in chunks
4 to 5 tablespoons olive oil
5 medium zucchini, unpeeled, sliced ¼-inch thick
1 large onion, sliced thin, separated into rings
3 medium, red-ripe tomatoes, each cut in 8 wedges
8 fresh mushrooms, rinsed and sliced
6 tablespoons chopped fresh parsley
Salt and pepper to taste
Seasoned dried bread crumbs (see note)
1 large clove garlic, minced

Brown eggplant lightly in about 2 tablespoons of the oil. Put vegetables in large deep casserole (2½ to 3 quart size) in 2 layers, starting with eggplant and ending with mushrooms and parsley. Season each vegetable with salt and pepper. Sprinkle bread crumbs on top, about ¼ cup, Mary Jane says. Mix garlic with the rest of the oil and pour over vegetables. Bake at 350°F., uncovered, for 1 hour.

*Mary Jane Von der Ahe*
*Studio City, California*

## NOTE

Packaged dried bread crumbs vary in seasonings. To season your own, add dried herbs, garlic salt, seasoning salt and Parmesan cheese, to your taste. A little marjoram, thyme, and tarragon or basil would be a nice combination here.

# Zucchini Fritti

4 to 6 servings

6 medium unpeeled zucchini, diced
3 onions, quartered, thinly sliced
½ cup corn oil
1 teaspoon garlic salt, or to taste
½ cup shredded mozzarella or Swiss cheese

Prepare zucchini and separate quartered onions into layers so you have thin slivers. In heavy pan, cook onions in heated oil slowly until soft and translucent. Add zucchini and stir-fry over moderate heat until lightly browned, just a few minutes. Add garlic salt to taste, mix well, and add cheese. Cover pan, turn off heat, and allow cheese to melt. Serve while zucchini is still crisp-tender.

*Angela Burkle*
*York, Pennsylvania*

# Sautéed Zucchini Vermouth

2 servings

Vary amount according to your family size or number of guests. For each two cups of sliced, unpeeled zucchini, melt 1½ tablespoons butter or margarine in a heavy saucepan. Add zucchini and stir over moderate heat until slices are shiny and coated with butter. Add 1 to 2 tablespoons dry Vermouth (the lesser amount for very tender, young zucchini), cover pan, and cook gently until just tender, 3 to 5 minutes. Shake pan often to prevent sticking. Season to taste with salt and pepper and sprinkle with 2 tablespoons freshly grated Parmesan or Romano cheese. Cover again and heat until cheese melts and flavors blend, about 1 minute.

*Susan Havekotte*
*Richardson, Texas*

# Zucchini Bake

This is not exactly a casserole and not quite a bread. It is an unusual dish with interesting flavor and is easy to make. We served it as a potato or rice replacement at a buffet supper.

6 servings

2 cups finely diced, unpeeled zucchini (can be larger,
    more mature zucchini)
½ cup finely chopped parsley
½ cup freshly grated Parmesan cheese
1 clove garlic, minced
¼ cup olive oil
3 eggs, beaten
Salt and pepper
¾ cup packaged biscuit mix

Mix together zucchini, parsley, cheese, garlic and olive oil. Stir in beaten eggs and season well with salt and pepper. Blend in biscuit mix until mixture is smooth. Spread in greased 8½-inch round or 9-inch square dish. Bake at 350°F. 35 to 40 minutes. Cut into wedges or squares and serve from baking dish.

*Virginia Gallagher*
*San Francisco, California*

## VARIATION

**Cocktail Zucchini Sticks:** Double the recipe for *Zucchini Bake* and season with chile powder or 4 tablespoons diced, seeded, canned green chiles. Spread in greased jelly roll pan and bake until browned, 25 to 30 minutes. Cut into fingers and serve warm, with drinks.

# Zucchini Frittata

Three Italian favorites—zucchini, prosciutto, and Parmesan cheese—make this easy-going omelet much more filling than the softer French omelet. Popular for breakfast, luncheon or supper.

4 generous servings

*4 to 6 small zucchini*
*3 tablespoons olive oil*
*2 tablespoons butter or margarine*
*8 eggs*
*1 teaspoon salt*
*Freshly ground black pepper to taste*
*½ cup freshly grated Parmesan cheese*
*3 ounces prosciutto (Italian ham), cut into small pieces*

Remove tips from unpeeled zucchini and slice thinly. In large heavy skillet, heat olive oil and butter together. Add zucchini and cook, stirring frequently, until tender and lightly tinged with brown, about 5 minutes. Beat eggs and season with salt and pepper and 2 tablespoons of the cheese. Pour over zucchini. Stir lightly, then cook over medium heat until omelet is set on the bottom but still soft looking on top, 4 to 5 minutes. Sprinkle with prosciutto and balance of Parmesan. Put under broiler a few minutes, until cheese is melted. Serve from pan, cut in wedges.

*Marva Tobler*
*Salt Lake City, Utah*

# Zucchini Green Chile Casserole

New Mexico cooks like their foods hot and zesty with chiles. Use the amount of green chiles that suits your own taste.

6 servings

2 pounds zucchini
Salt
1 large onion, chopped
1 clove garlic, chopped
2 tablespoons butter or margarine
Pepper
½ teaspoon dried oregano leaves
Pinch of ground cumin
1 can (14½ ounces) tomatoes (see note)
2 cups grated, sharp cheddar cheese
Chopped canned or frozen (defrosted)
   green chiles to taste
1 cup lightly crushed corn chips

Slice unpeeled zucchini and place in heavy saucepan with ½ inch boiling salted water. Cover and simmer gently until tender, about 10 minutes. Drain, if necessary, and turn into large buttered casserole. Sauté onion and garlic in melted butter until soft and add to zucchini. Sprinkle with salt and pepper, oregano and cumin. Break up tomatoes with fingers and stir into dish along with cheese and 1 to 4 tablespoons chiles. Top with crushed chips. Bake in slow oven (325°F.) 45 minutes to 1 hour.

*Mary Reinhart*
*Albuquerque, New Mexico*

**NOTE**

Mrs. Reinhart uses canned tomatoes packed with green chiles, which may not be available in your area—and are usually very hot—and ½ cup chopped green chiles.

171

# Zucchini Cheese Loaf

This light, non-meat loaf may be served as a main dish or to accompany fish, chicken, lamb chops, and such. It is good with grilled tomatoes, French bread and fruit.

6 to 8 servings

4 medium, unpeeled zucchini, cut in chunks
1 onion, cut in pieces
1 green bell pepper, cut in pieces, seeded
2 cups soda cracker crumbs
Salt and freshly ground black pepper
2 eggs, lightly beaten
⅓ cup salad oil
¾ cup grated cheddar cheese
2 to 4 tablespoons grated Parmesan cheese
Paprika

In blender, food chopper, or food processor, grind together (but do not purée) the zucchini, onion and green pepper. Do in several batches if blender is used. Stir in cracker crumbs and season to taste with salt and pepper. Gently stir in eggs, salad oil and cheddar. Spread in loaf pan (9 x 5 x 3 inches) and sprinkle with Parmesan to cover, and paprika. Bake at 325°F. 45 to 55 minutes, until firm. Cut into slices and serve hot.

Betty Crowe
Los Angeles, California

# Zucchini Walnut Bread

A moist nut bread that's a favorite with all the zucchini fanciers.

2 loaves

2 cups grated, unpeeled zucchini
(about 2 or 3 medium)
1 cup raisins
3 cups unbleached white flour
1 teaspoon soda
1 teaspoon salt
¾ teaspoon baking powder
1 tablespoon cinnamon
4 eggs
2 cups sugar
1 cup vegetable oil
2 teaspoons grated lemon peel
1 cup chopped walnuts

Prepare grated zucchini and set aside. Rinse raisins, drain, and mix with 2 tablespoons of the flour. Sift flour with soda, salt, baking powder and cinnamon. Beat eggs and gradually beat in the sugar, then the oil. With rubber spatula, blend in dry ingredients alternately with grated zucchini. When thoroughly mixed, stir in raisins, lemon peel and nuts. Turn into 2 greased and floured loaf pans (9 x 5 x 3 inches). Bake at 350°F. about 55 minutes, or until top springs back when lightly touched. Cool in pans about 10 minutes, then turn out on wire racks to cool.

Mrs. Harry B. Thomas
York, Pennsylvania

# Lemon Zucchini Cookies

These delicate soft lemon cookies have the extra goodness of fresh grated zucchini.

6 to 7 dozen

*1 cup grated unpeeled zucchini (1 to 2 medium)*
*2 cups all-purpose flour*
*½ teaspoon salt*
*1 teaspoon baking powder*
*¾ cup butter or margarine*
*¾ cup sugar*
*1 egg, beaten*
*1 teaspoon grated fresh lemon peel*
*1 cup chopped walnuts*
*Lemon Frost (optional)*

Grate zucchini and sift flour with salt and baking powder. Cream together butter and sugar. Beat in egg and lemon peel. Stir in flour until dough is smooth, then blend in zucchini and nuts. Drop from rounded teaspoon onto greased cookie sheet in mounds about 1½ inches across and ½ inch thick. Bake at 375°F. 15 to 20 minutes. Cookies brown only lightly. While hot, drizzle with *Lemon Frost*, if you wish. Cool on wire racks.

## Lemon Frost

Blend together 1 cup powdered sugar and about 1½ tablespoons fresh lemon juice.

*Eloise Ellis*
*Salt Lake City, Utah*

# Zucchini Nut Cakes

Mrs. Morehead bakes this in small loaf pans for holiday gifts. Moist, spicy, and laced with nuts.

2 loaf cakes

2 cups grated unpeeled zucchini (*about 3 medium*)
2 cups all-purpose flour
2 teaspoons soda
½ teaspoon baking powder
1 teaspoon salt
3 teapoons cinnamon
3 eggs
2 cups sugar
¾ cup light salad oil
1 cup coarsely chopped walnuts
   (Mrs. Morehead often uses more, she says)

Prepare zucchini and sift flour with soda, baking powder, salt and cinnamon. With electric mixer, beat eggs until very light and fluffy. Beat in sugar and oil, then blend in dry mixture and zucchini. Stir in nuts. Turn batter into 2 greased and floured small loaf pans (about 7½ x 4½ x 2½ inches—fruit-cake size) or 1 8-inch bundt cake pan. Bake at 350°F. 45 to 50 minutes (about 1 hour for bundt pan) or until center springs back when touched lightly. Cool in pans about 5 minutes, then turn out on wire racks to cool. Sprinkle bundt cake with sifted powdered sugar if you wish or drizzle with the *Lemon Glaze* or *Orange Glaze* (see index). These keep beautifully in the refrigerator, wrapped in foil.

*Lelamay Morehead*
*Morgan Hill, California*

175

# Swiss Carrot Torte

This elegant dessert was first introduced to Americans years ago by distinguished writer and cook Helen McCully, food editor of *House Beautiful*. It has been a favorite of mine and of our guests ever since. Thank you, Helen, for allowing me to share this with my readers.

8 servings

¾ cup fine dry bread crumbs
plus extra crumbs for pan
⅔ cup firmly packed, grated
raw carrots
(3 to 4 medium)
1⅔ cups unblanched almonds

½ teaspoon cinnamon
¼ teaspoon ground cloves
6 eggs, separated
1¼ cups sugar
1 large lemon, grated peel and juice
Lemon Glaze

Grease an 8-inch spring-form pan (with removable bottom) and line bottom with waxed paper. Grease paper and coat bottom and sides with about 2 tablespoons fine dry bread crumbs. Prepare carrots and grind almonds to a find dry powder (do a half cup at a time, if done in blender). Mix almonds with carrots, ¾ cup crumbs, and spices, in a large mixing bowl. In separate bowl or mixer, beat yolks, sugar, grated lemon peel and juice until they look thick, light and creamy. Beat whites until they hold a peak. Stir yolks into carrot mixture, then gently fold in whites until white patches disappear. Spoon into prepared pan and bake at 350°F. 45 minutes to 1 hour, until cake tester is clean and dry when stuck into center of cake. Cool and remove from pan. Wrap in foil or plastic wrap and refrigerate 2 or 3 days to mellow the flavors before serving. Spoon *Lemon Glaze* over the top and decorate cake with freshly grated carrot.

## Lemon Glaze

Combine 2 cups sifted powdered sugar with the juice of a lemon and a little water, if needed, to make glaze pourable. A little lemon zest may be added, if you like.

Helen McCully
New York, New York

# Almond Carrot Cake

Different from any of the other carrot cakes I've tried, this cake was worked out by my neighbor, good cook, and fellow needlepointer, Margaret Buttrey. Please note, the ½ cup of oil is correct! I doubted it until I tried this recipe.

1 large sheet cake

1 cup slivered, blanched almonds
2 cups grated raw carrots
1 can (8 ounces) crushed pineapple,
   well drained
1 cup flaked coconut
1 cup all-purpose flour
1 cup whole wheat flour
1½ cups sugar
1 teaspoon soda

2 teaspoons cinnamon
½ teaspoon nutmeg
½ teaspoon salt
3 eggs
½ cup oil
¾ cup buttermilk
2 teaspoons vanilla
Buttermilk Glaze

Combine almonds, carrots, pineapple and coconut. Blend together in plastic bag or put through sifter the flours, sugar, soda, spices and salt. In large bowl, beat eggs with oil, buttermilk and vanilla. Add flour mixture all at once and stir until blended. Blend in carrot mixture. Turn into a greased and floured pan (9 x 13 x 2 inches). Bake at 350°F. for 45 minutes or until pick inserted near center comes out clean. Prick hot cake with a fork at ½-inch intervals and slowly drizzle with *Buttermilk Glaze*. Cool. Serve from pan, cut in squares.

## Buttermilk Glaze

Combine in saucepan ⅔ cup sugar, ½ cup buttermilk, and ⅓ cup butter or margarine. Heat to boiling and boil 5 minutes. Add ½ teaspoon vanilla.

*Margaret Buttrey*
*Hollywood, California*

177

# Great Grandma's Sheep-Wagon Carrot Cake

"Sturdy little pioneer cake," the contributor wrote, "And often served warm for breakfast." She insists the 12-hour soaking period improves the quality of the cake. We agree.

2 loaf cakes or 1 8-inch tube cake

1⅓ cups sugar
1⅓ cups water
1 cup raisins (or half raisins and half
   chopped mixed candied fruits)
1 tablespoon butter or margarine
2 large, finely grated carrots (about 1½ cups)
1 teaspoon cinnamon
1 teaspoon ground cloves
1 teaspoon nutmeg
2½ cups all-purpose flour
½ teaspoon salt
1 teaspoon soda
2 teaspoons baking powder
1 cup chopped walnuts

Combine sugar, water, raisins, butter, carrots, and spices in medium-size saucepan. Heat to boiling, then reduce heat and simmer for 5 minutes. Cover and let stand overnight or for 12 hours. Sift together flour, salt, soda and baking powder and stir into fruit mixture. Add walnuts and stir until batter is well mixed. Turn into 2 small greased and floured loaf pans (8 x 4½ x 2 inches) or 1 tube pan. Bake at 275°F. for 2 hours. Cool in pans for 10 minutes, then turn out onto wire racks to cool.

### NOTE

Cake may be baked at 325°F. for about 1½ hours, or until tops spring back when touched lightly.

*Louise Frye*
*Morgan Hill, California*

178

# Golden Carrot Pie

Honey gives a lovely, inimitable flavor to this pie that's somewhat like pumpkin yet deliciously different.

6 to 8 servings

1 unbaked 9-inch pastry shell
2 cups sieved or puréed cooked carrots
1 cup mild flavored honey, such as clover or orange
¾ cup undiluted evaporated milk
½ teaspoon salt
1 teaspoon cinnamon
½ teaspoon nutmeg
½ teaspoon ground ginger
1/8 teaspoon ground cloves
3 eggs, slightly beaten

Chill pastry shell while you make filling. Combine carrots, honey, milk, salt, and spices. Stir in slightly beaten eggs, blend well, and pour into pastry shell. Bake in 400°F. oven 40 to 45 minutes, until knife inserted near edge of pie comes out clean. Filling may be slightly quivery in center. Cool on wire rack 30 minutes, then chill. Top each serving with lightly whipped cream, sour cream or ice cream, if you wish.

*Mona Schafer*
*Whittier, California*

# Index